Fiori di Zucca

VALENTINA HARRIS

Fiori di Zucca

dbp

DUNCAN BAIRD PUBLISHERS

LONDON

Fiori di Zucca
Valentina Harris

Distributed in the USA and Canada by
Sterling Publishing Co., Inc.
387 Park Avenue South
New York, NY 10016-8810

First published in the UK and USA in 2013 by
Duncan Baird Publishers, an imprint of
Watkins Publishing Ltd
Sixth Floor
75 Wells Street
London, England W1T 3QH

A member of Osprey Group

Managing Editor: Grace Cheetham
Editors: Nicola Graimes, Wanda Whitely and Jo Murray
Managing Designer: Manisha Patel
Design and photography art direction: Gabriella Le Grazie
Americanizer: Beverly LeBlanc
Production: Uzma Taj
Commissioned photography: William Lingwood
Food Stylists: Lucy McKelvie and Valentina Harris
Prop Stylist: Lucy Harvey

ISBN: 978-1-84899-085-2

10 9 8 7 6 5 4 3 2 1

Typeset in ITC Berkeley Old Style
Color reproduction by Colorscan
Printed in Thailand

This book is for all the storytellers around my table over the years, and to all those amazing people who taught me to cook, respect and understand food—I will never forget you and what you gave me.

Author's acknowledgments

I would like to thank Heather, Grace, Wanda, Nicky, Jo
and everyone else who helped me bring my stories and
recipes to life.

Just in case you were wondering, Fiori di Zucca means
zucchini or pumpkin flowers, but the word zucca is also
used affectionately to mean one's own head. In this case
perhaps, the alternative 'Flowers from my Head'
translation has an appropriately personal feel.

Publisher's note: While every care has been taken in compiling
the recipes for this book, Duncan Baird Publishers, or any other
persons who have been involved in working on this publication,
cannot accept responsibility for any errors or omissions,
inadvertent or not, that might be found in the recipes or text, nor
for any problems that might arise as a result of preparing one
of these recipes. If you are pregnant or breastfeeding or have any
special dietary requirements or medical conditions, it is advisable
to consult a medical professional before following any of the
recipes contained in this book.

Notes on the Recipes
Unless otherwise stated:
Use large eggs and medium fruit and vegetables
Use fresh ingredients, including herbs and chilies
Flour should be measured by spooning it into the cup measure
and leveling the surface
Use fresh ingredients, including herbs and chilies
1 tsp. = 5ml 1 tbsp. = 15ml 1 cup = 240ml

TWENTY STORIES, EIGHTY-FIVE RECIPES FROM TEN COUNTRIES

Me, aged 3, at La Tambura.

INTRODUCTION

Over the past thirty years, I have made my living as an Italian food expert, writer, teacher and chef. When I speak, however, I don't sound remotely Italian. The accent is missing, but nevertheless Italy and Italian cooking remain firmly in my heart. If it is true you can only really become acquainted with a place through your taste buds, then it is Italy I have got to know best in the course of my life.

I have wanted to write this book for a very long time. It is a collection of my family's stories dating back to the fifteenth century, all connected to family recipes. Some of the stories and recipes in this book originate from Rome, some from Tuscany, while others come from such far-flung places as Russia, Serbia, Belgium, Turkey, Paris, Provence, Morocco, China and America. Every ingredient used in these recipes has made me who I am, both as a cook and as a person.

I am the youngest daughter of an Anglo/Irish Dutchman and an Italian/Belgian mother. Born in Peking in 1914, my mother's lineage as a noblewoman of the Italian Sforza dynasty and distant cousin to the Belgian royal family made her very blue-blooded indeed. But this was sprinkled with a hint of exoticism through some Russian blood.

My fine, upstanding English army officer father met my lovely, elegant Italian countess mother in Italy at the end of World War II, and they fell madly, deeply and inextricably in love. They settled in Italy, and my father gave up his English life and family for the love of my mother. Their union, which scandalized Italian society because my father was divorced and not a Roman Catholic, effectively brought my Italian grandfather's impressive political career to an end.

By the time I was seven or so, Dad realized there was not a lot about my three older brothers or me that was obviously English. Growing up in Italy, with only brief periods spent living in England, we seemed to have little understanding of the principle of the stiff upper lip, refused to comprehend the rules of cricket, could never speak without waving our hands and wore our over-emotional, sensitive hearts firmly on our sleeves! Dad decided it was his duty to instil in us something unmistakably English, and set about teaching us to sound as English as possible (hence the lack of an Italian accent), with the aid of the BBC World Service and his beloved shortwave radio. It worked perfectly. I sound like an English BBC Radio 4 presenter, while feeling in my heart and soul I am Italian. I dream, work out my problems, curse, kiss and always cook in Italian, even if I am making a curry!

Central to many of my stories and recipes in this book is a very special house in Tuscany that will always be home to me. Although, sadly, it is no longer mine to own, within the pages of this book it remains forever mine to love. The house is called La Tambura. It was also home to our caretaker, Beppino, the man who not only taught me how to cook, but also gave me the understanding of how food is grown and produced. Without Beppino, I would never have chosen to make a living out of cooking or writing, teaching and presenting about food.

Most of my early life—the period that is covered in these stories—was spent between the village of Ronchi, on the northern Tuscan coast where La Tambura is located, and the luscious, exuberant city of Rome. My parents, Howard and Fiammetta, lived permanently in Tuscany in their later years, but before that we spent only holidays and long weekends at the house, often joined by other family members and friends of all ages and nationalities. There never seemed to be fewer than twenty people around the table at any meal at La Tambura.

Many of these stories are the same ones that I was told during those family mealtimes, stories I have retold many times subsequently. Now they are in print for the very first time. It is with great pride and joy that I share the stories and the food of my life, and hope very much you will take pleasure from these pages as you read my memoir and try my recipes.

Clockwise from top: Il Duca Francesco Sforza;
my Nonno Carlo (pictured right) with
a great uncle; and my great grandmother.

1.   A STORY OF FAMILY FOLKLORE: HOW THE *Sforzas* FOUGHT FOR MILAN

This is a tale about my mother Fiammetta's ancestors, the Sforzas. It is a story my father would regale us with at the dinner table at our Tuscan home, La Tambura. That long, long table was always set with a beautiful, spotlessly clean and very colorful tablecloth. We had matching napkins, each one in its special napkin ring so we could always identify our own. There would be a bright bowl of zinnias from the garden, our lovely caramel-colored china, shiny octagonal tumblers with a dark blue rim for water and wine and the heavy, well-worn family silverware, complete with the Sforza family crest. Dad would only tell the story when he was feeling particularly flirtatious toward my mother, his brown eyes flashing, laughter rumbling in his chest. She would smile back in that enigmatic way she saved only for him.

I am almost certain this tale of the Sforzas is one of those that, over time, has absorbed elements of other stories. Its location and cast of characters might well have been changed at the whim of more than one narrator to make the tale more dramatic and engaging. I do know, however, that these characters existed, and that I am related to them—albeit distantly. And, although I cannot vouch for its historical accuracy, I love retelling the tale. I believe that insisting on the absolute truth from one's best memories sometimes only serves to steal away part of their enjoyment.

The story is set in the fifteenth century during a battle between the Sforzas and a second Milanese noble family. It was at the time of Ludovico Sforza, Duke of Milan, a man who, like all the Sforzas, governed by force and power-politics. My mother's ancestors were warriors—not bankers, like many of their contemporaries, such as the Medici.

My mother's ancestors were warriors—not bankers, like many of their contemporaries, such as the Medici.

It was during this especially bloody battle, in which the family's castle was besieged, that one of the noble Sforza ladies appeared on the ramparts. Covered in filth and with wild hair, she brandished her sword and, eyes flashing with hatred, she stood glaring down at the enemy. From below, the leader called out to her, "Desist madam. Give up now or we shall be forced to take your children!" In reply, she waved her skirts at the soldiers, shouting lewdly, "Never mind! Go ahead if you want to, there'll be plenty more before you know it!"

Later, after a truce had been agreed, a banquet was held in the great hall of the Castello Sforzesco (which can still be visited in Milan today and even has its own Metro station). As the guests sat down to roasted haunch of wild boar, wood pigeon and other fine dishes, they had no idea what their hosts had in store for them. They were satisfied good manners and noble protocol were being observed, but they should have been on their guard: the Sforzas were infamously treacherous. (At this point in the story my father would give my mother a funny look, smoothing his thumb over the engraved family crest on his knife handle—a rampant lion holding the branch of a quince tree.) As soon as the guests had raised their goblets in a toast, a group of crack assassins, whom the Duke had hidden behind the tapestries in the banqueting hall, leapt out and dragged the guests away to face a grisly end. The rest of the party continued with the feast, calmly, as if nothing had happened.

At the end of the story, my father would lift his own wine glass and drink, never once taking his eyes off my mother. Depending upon who was there, and whether they had heard the story before, slightly shocked laughter might ripple around the table while my mother flashed my dad another of her enigmatic looks before changing the conversation.

Ludovico Sforza ruled Milan from 1489 to 1508. He famously defeated Louis XII's army at the Battle of Fornovo, with weapons made from the seventy tons of bronze that had been intended for a statue of himself he had commissioned from Leonardo da Vinci. Ludovico il Moro, as he was also known, was the artist's patron, and his tomb lies in the church that houses *The Last Supper*, which the Duke had also commissioned. Through Ludovico's power and patronage, he left an important political and cultural legacy to Milan at the time of the Renaissance.

I also like to think of my ancestor Ludovico as the unsung hero responsible in part for the creation of one of the most traditional dishes of Lombardy, the ubiquitous risotto. By 1550, rice fields occupied over 550 hectares of land in the Dukedom of Milan, thanks to Ludovico's decision

Castello Sforzesco Milano.

to flood the area to enable the tender plants to grow in water. His intricate and brilliantly engineered irrigation system is still largely in use today on the flat, wet plains of western Lombardy and eastern Piedmont. For almost five centuries, rice for making risotto has been the main crop grown in the area, with many different varieties being introduced over that period to create this remarkable dish in all its wonderful forms.

It seems inevitable—with Ludovico Sforza as my forebear— that I should have fallen in love with the slow, steady ritual of making risotto. When I was just four or five

All afternoon, Beppino and I checked, tasted and skimmed the chicken stock as it bubbled away.

years old, Beppino, the caretaker at our house, La Tambura, taught me how to make it. Long before I discovered the historical link between the dish and my ancestor, I cared about risotto passionately. But now that I know the link is there, it makes perfect sense I have always so loved eating and making the divinely decadent, velvety treat that is a properly made risotto.

The first time I made risotto with Beppino, he took me through the important rules of making *brodo*, the all-important stock. I remember us choosing the chicken, slaughtering it humanely, then gutting and plucking it. While it was being simmered for hours in salted water with celery, onions and carrot, a beef marrowbone and a meaty veal knuckle, I was given the all-important job of checking and cleaning the rice grains, which were delivered in large hessian sacks every fall from the Sforza rice fields near the small Tuscan town of Pontedera. Beppino measured out exactly how much rice we needed into a wide, shallow bowl—one fistful per person—and then I pored over it, picking out scraps of chaff and imperfect grains until all that remained was perfectly clean white rice.

All afternoon, Beppino and I checked, tasted and skimmed the chicken stock as it bubbled away. When it was done, he saved me my favorite bit: the chewy gizzard. For himself, he set aside the veal knuckle and the marrowbone. We ate them with our fingers, sitting side by side on the marble back doorstep of the house, a small saucer of sea salt between us. Beppino often told me stories of the time he was a chef at the famous Ristorante Savini, in the Galleria in Milan, where he was responsible for the risotto. (Many years later,

I was to discover my favorite risotto-themed legend. This involved a sixteenth-century master of the stained glass windows at the Duomo in Milan, and the keen workman he put in charge of painting the yellow sections of the glorious windows in the third chapel past the transept. In those days, ground saffron diluted in water was used to color the glass. The workman was so passionate about his saffron powder that he was nicknamed Zafferano by his colleagues, who claimed one day he would end up putting it into his risotto. And one day he did: on the occasion of the wedding of the master's daughter, he presented two tureens of the golden, saffron-scented risotto as a wedding gift, which was carried into the feast by a pair of pages and accompanied by a triumphant bugle fanfare.)

The stock finished and the dishwashing done, with Beppino standing at my shoulder and my feet planted firmly on a chair in front of the stove, I began to make my first risotto. Beppino taught me the importance of using the right-shaped saucepan, of chopping the onion so finely it vanishes into the background of the risotto, of frying the onion so it becomes completely soft without coloring and of bravely adding the rice all in one go. Then, carefully, we took the risotto through all its processes. I would give myself up to the rhythm of the recipe, allowing the rice itself to tell me what to do and when to do it, knowing somehow, even then, that Beppino might not always be there to prompt me whenever I made risotto, but that his voice would always guide me.

First, *la tentazione*: the long, slow, careful toasting of the rice grains without browning, so the heat from the pan permeates right through each grain evenly, sealing off the inner core to prevent overcooking later, once the liquid is added.

> I would give myself up to the rhythm of the recipe, allowing the rice itself to tell me what to do and when to do it...

Then, *il sospiro*: the addition of the first liquid, the satisfying rush of steam and the audible sighing of the rice as it drowns in pleasure, quivers in anticipation, settles again and finally begins to swell.

This is followed by long, leisurely, gentle stirring, waiting for the rice to beg for more hot stock after each addition, until it is time to remove it from the heat, add the last of the butter and cheese and cover the pot tightly. This guarantees the final process, *la mantecatura* (the essential creaming and stirring to incorporate air into the risotto), can take place just before serving.

I can still remember so clearly Beppino standing at the stove, patiently nursing his *brodo*. Whenever I was ill he would make me his version of the classic *Zuppa Pavese* (Pavese Soup, see page 19). I have always loved the story of how this soup was supposedly created. In Lombardy, in 1525, on the very day that King Francis I of France was defeated by Emperor Charles V of the Holy Roman Empire, the king declared, "Everything is lost except our honor." This was, however, not strictly true as the king had certainly not lost his appetite. He is said to have stormed around the Pavese countryside in desperate search for something to eat. Finally, he came upon a farm where a peasant woman was making soup. The king told her who he was and that he was very hungry. The woman placed a piece of old bread in a bowl and covered it with broth poured from her battered ladle. Then, thinking this food was not noble enough for a king—even one who had been so ignominiously defeated—she went to her henhouse, gathered two eggs and broke them into his soup bowl. Since then, the recipe has become much more sophisticated and elegant, but I love to remember the story of its noble origins, in much the same way as I remember with fondness and gratitude Beppino and my forebear, Ludvico Sforza, when I make one of my most favorite dishes, risotto.

Castello Sforzesco.

PARMESAN & BUTTER RISOTTO

Long before I discovered a historical link between risotto and my ancestor Ludovico Sforza, I fell in love with this simple dish. This recipe is ideal for beginners because it is easy to observe the changes in appearance and texture of the rice grains during the whole cooking process. To make a successful risotto, the pan used should be deep enough so the liquid does not evaporate too quickly, be heavy-based to allow the cooking process to be relatively slow and must have a lid that fits tightly. You can also add all sorts of other ingredients to this basic recipe, such as herbs, cooked pancetta, chicken or whatever takes your fancy.

Serves 6
Preparation time: 10 minutes, plus 4 minutes resting
Cooking time: 35 to 40 minutes

5 tablespoons unsalted butter
1 onion, finely chopped
2½ cups risotto rice, preferably vialone nano

6½ cups good-quality chicken, meat or vegetable stock, hot
1 cup freshly grated Parmesan cheese
kosher salt and freshly ground black pepper

Heat half the butter in a deep, heavy-based saucepan over very low heat. Add the onion and fry 10 minutes, or until the onion is soft but not colored. Increase the heat slightly to medium-low, add the rice and toast the grains 4 to 8 minutes, stirring, until they are opaque but not colored.

Add a ladleful of the hot stock and stir it in, letting the rice hiss and tremble as it absorbs the liquid. Continue adding the stock 2 ladlefuls at a time, stirring continuously with a wooden spoon and allowing the liquid to be absorbed. Do not add more stock until the spoon draws a clear wake behind it as you draw it through the rice. Cook about 20 minutes, or until the rice is creamy but still firm in the middle.

Remove the pan from the heat, stir in the Parmesan and remaining butter and season with salt and pepper. Cover and leave to rest 4 minutes, then stir again and serve.

PIEDMONTESE RISOTTO

This recipe reflects an earlier style of making risotto—as it would have been made in my ancestor's Ludovico's time—before the habit of toasting the rice grains in the *soffritto* (gently sautéed chopped onion and other vegetables) was introduced. It is meant to be quite soupy and wet, and should therefore be served in deep soup plates or bowls. Preferably use carnaroli rice, which is from the Piedmont region.

Serves 6
Preparation time: 10 minutes, plus 4 minutes resting
Cooking time: 25 minutes

8¾ cups good-quality beef or veal stock
2½ cups risotto rice, preferably carnaroli

heaped ½ cup freshly grated Parmesan cheese
4 tablespoons unsalted butter
2 ounces finely shaved white or black truffle, or heaped 1 tablespoon truffle butter
kosher salt
freshly grated nutmeg, to serve

Put the stock in a large saucepan and bring to a boil. Stir in the rice and return to a boil, then turn the heat down and simmer 20 minutes, stirring occasionally, or until the rice is creamy, but still firm in the middle.

Remove the pan from the heat and stir in the Parmesan, butter and truffle. Season with salt, to taste. Cover and leave to rest 4 minutes, then stir again and serve with a little nutmeg grated over the top.

CLASSIC MILANESE RISOTTO

Traditionally, bone marrow is used in this recipe, but you can leave it out if you prefer, adding an extra 3 tablespoons butter instead. As the dish is from Lombardy, the cheese used is Grana Padano, not Parmigiano Reggiano; and saffron powder is more often used throughout Italy than the strands.

Serves 4 to 6
Preparation time: 15 minutes,
   plus 10 minutes soaking and
   4 minutes resting
Cooking time: 30 minutes

½ white or brown onion, very finely
   chopped
7 tablespoons unsalted butter
3 tablespoons chopped raw beef bone
   marrow (optional)

2 cups risotto rice, preferably vialone
   gigante or carnaroli
6½ cups strong veal, beef and/or
   chicken stock, hot
⅛ teaspoon saffron powder
½ cup freshly grated Grana Padano
   cheese, plus extra to serve

Put the onion in a bowl, cover with cold water and leave to soak 10 minutes. (This softens the flavor of the onion and makes it sweeter, but this step is optional.) Drain the onion and squeeze it dry in a clean dish towel.

Heat half the butter in a deep, heavy-based pan over low heat. Add the onion and beef marrow, if using, and fry gently 10 minutes, or until the onion is soft but not colored. Increase the heat to medium, add the rice and stir thoroughly to coat it in the butter mixture until crackling hot but not colored.

Add a ladleful of hot stock and stir it in, letting the rice hiss and tremble as it absorbs the liquid. Continue adding the stock, a ladleful at a time, and cook over medium-low heat 10 minutes, stirring continuously and letting all the liquid be absorbed before adding more.

Stir in the saffron powder and continue to cook as before 10 minutes longer, or until the rice is creamy but still firm in the middle.

Remove the pan from the heat and stir in the remaining butter and the Grana Padano. Cover the pan and leave to rest 4 minutes, then stir again and serve with extra grated Grana Padano for adding at the table.

PAVESE SOUP

This is my version of the classic soup Beppino would make for me as
a child when I was feeling unwell. It never failed to make me feel better.

Serves 6
Preparation time: 30 minutes,
  plus cooling
Cooking time: 2½ hours

6 tablespoons unsalted butter
2 tablespoons vegetable oil
6 slices Italian-style bread
6 eggs
3 ounces Grana Padano cheese,
  freshly grated, plus extra to serve
kosher salt and freshly ground
  black pepper

Chicken broth:
1 large ready-to-cook boiling fowl
  or chicken, with giblets
2 carrots, trimmed
2 onions, halved
2 celery sticks
2 tomatoes, halved
2 cabbage or large lettuce leaves
1 handful of parsley sprigs

First, make the broth. Rinse the chicken and giblets under cold running water, then put them
in a large saucepan with all the remaining broth ingredients. Pour in 2½ quarts water and add
a little salt. Bring to a boil, then turn the heat down to low and simmer gently, part-covered,
2 hours. Remove the pan from the heat and leave to cool completely. Once cold, remove the
chicken and giblets from the broth and discard. Strain the liquid through a fine strainer into
a large bowl. Leave the broth to stand, then remove any fat from the surface and strain again.
If not using immediately, cover, chill and use within 3 days or freeze up to 1 month.

Heat the oven to 350°F. Pour 6½ cups of the strained broth into a saucepan and bring
to a gentle simmer. Meanwhile, melt the butter with the oil in a large skillet over medium
heat. Add the bread slices and fry on both sides until golden and crisp. Remove from the pan
and drain on paper towels.

Put a slice of fried bread into each of six ovenproof bowls and make a hollow in the bread
with the back of a spoon. Crack an egg into the hollow in each slice, being careful not
to break the yolk. Sprinkle each egg with the Grana Padano and season with salt and pepper.

Carefully ladle the very hot broth onto and around the eggs. The extreme heat of the broth
should just cook the eggs. If the eggs are not cooked to your liking, put the bowls on a cookie
sheet and put in the oven 2 minutes to set the eggs a little bit more. Serve the soup with extra
grated Grana Padano for adding at the table.

STUFFED WOOD PIGEON

In Lombardy, stuffed wood pigeon was once the preferred dish of the nobility, and the origins of this dish date back to the early Renaissance. If you can't find bitter almonds, use hard amaretti cookies or simmer a handful of blanched almonds in water with a leaf from an artichoke plant 10 minutes before draining and drying. The stuffing can also be used in chicken and guinea fowl.

Serves 4
Preparation time: 40 minutes,
   plus 25 minutes standing and
   5 minutes resting
Cooking time: 45 minutes

4 prepared large, plump wood
   pigeons, with livers
7 tablespoons unsalted butter
1 small onion, finely chopped
1 cup fresh white bread crumbs
1 egg, beaten
2 bitter almonds, chopped, or
   2 amaretti cookies, finely crumbled

⅓ cup freshly grated Grana Padano
   cheese
½ cup chicken or game stock
⅓ cup olive oil
1 rosemary sprig, needles roughly
   chopped
scant ½ cup dry white wine
kosher salt and freshly ground
   black pepper
watercress and chargrilled polenta,
   to serve

Dress the pigeons, if necesssary, removing any tiny quills, and leave to one side. Carefully clean and trim the livers.

To make the stuffing, melt one-third of the butter in a large skillet over medium heat. Add the livers and onion and fry 4 to 5 minutes until brown and the onion is very soft. Spoon the mixture into a blender with the bread crumbs, egg, almonds, Grana Padano and half of the stock. Blend briefly to make a coarse paste, adding more stock, if necessary. Leave to stand 20 minutes, then season with salt and pepper.

Heat the oven to 350°F. Fill the cavity of each pigeon with the stuffing, then sew or tie the pigeons closed with kitchen string, or use small metal skewers.

Pour the oil into a baking dish, lay the pigeons in the oil and spread the remaining butter over the breast of each bird. Add the rosemary, wine and any remaining stock. Roast 40 minutes, basting frequently, or until the pigeons are cooked through. Leave to rest 5 minutes, then remove the string or skewers. Serve with watercress and chargrilled polenta.

Me with Nonna Valentine.

2. MY RUSSIAN ANCESTRESS, *Valentina*

When I was a child, my grandmother Valentine told me we were both named after another Valentina, our mysterious Russian ancestress. How we were related to her was a mystery—my Nonna did not even know her full name—but I nevertheless reveled in stories about her. Valentina was wild, spirited and died young, and those facts alone had the power to thrill, with their suggestion of adventure, rebellion, romance and tragedy.

There was always a hint of scandal in Nonna's stories about Valentina. As one might expect from her passionate and wayward nature, she loved to flirt with men and, delighting in their company, was prepared to flout convention and dispense with the formality of having a chaperone whenever she felt like it. Although such behavior would have shocked the more upstanding members of Russian society in the 1700s, there were still plenty of people who flocked to her sumptuous banquets. Valentina, a lively hostess, was nothing if not generous, and the feasts she provided were reputed to be truly fabulous. She would serve sparkling platters of shattered ice topped with pearly gray caviar and piles of soft, warm blini; tender, succulent shashlik served on long, sword-shaped skewers; poussins roasted in a type of sour cream; plump *piroshki* (small Russian pies); marinated fish with pickles; and smoked meats. There were two dishes, apparently, that were always served at her parties and known to be her favorites: braised duck with cinnamon, and a plum and nut tart.

> She would serve sparkling platters of shattered ice topped with pearly gray caviar and piles of soft, warm blini...

My Russian ancestress loved eating game, especially if she had bagged it herself. She frequently rode out hunting, accompanied by her adoring companions. Dazzlingly elegant in a beautifully cut riding habit, Valentina galloped side-saddle across the Russian countryside for hours on end. She was renowned as a fearless and accomplished horsewoman.

I am certain that the story of Valentina's unhappy demise has been embellished over the years. My grandmother, who loved to recount the tale, might well have been one of those who did so—not that it mattered to me. It happened on a very cold winter's day. The determined and courageous Valentina set out for a long day's duck shooting with a group of male companions. Warmed by copious amounts of vodka, which they consumed to protect them against the chill, they galloped across the flat, frosty landscape, and for the first few hours all went well.

Then Valentina started to feel very unwell. She did not have a lady-in-waiting with her whom she could call on to unlace her complicated bodice—or, indeed, anywhere private in which to do it—so, although she felt breathless and faint, Valentina rode on. While the men happily called a halt from time to time, dismounting to relieve themselves behind a tree, Valentina stayed mounted throughout, never once betraying the extreme discomfort that she was feeling.

If she could only have got home sooner, Valentina might have survived. Instead, her companions, wishing to work up an appetite for the evening's feasting ahead, were keen to carry on riding for several hours longer. It was said that Valentina continued to smile and toss her head, exchanging jokes and shouts of delight with her fellow horsemen, although, by now, she was gravely ill. She remained on her horse until the bitter end; and it was only when she dismounted that she collapsed. She died in the arms of one of her male companions.

I think about Valentina, the Russian ancestress, from time to time. There is not a single picture of her anywhere among the family memorabilia, and I would love to find out more about her, but, without anything more than a first name to go by, I know my search would be fruitless. One item of hers does remain, however, and it is very precious to me. As a child, I was given a little gold pin that Valentina was wearing, reputedly, on that fateful day. It is one of those long, slender brooches that are used to hold the frills of a lace stock in place, and from it hangs a tiny Russian bear. I wear it often, to remember the woman who gave me my name—and, quite possibly, my rebellious streak. I also attribute my passion for caviar, which I must surely have acquired from someone, to Valentina.

*Three generations: Nonna Valentine, me and
my mother, Fiammetta, on Christmas-day.*

BRAISED CINNAMON DUCK WITH CARAMELIZED PEARS

This dish was created by my mother. She called it *"alla Valentina Russa"* in memory of our ancestress, because she felt it had a Russian feel. Perhaps she was right and it is similar to the braised duck Valentina might have served.

Serves 4
Preparation time: 15 minutes
Cooking time: 2½ hours

1 teaspoon kosher salt
1 large oven-ready duck, about
  4 pounds, jointed
2 tablespoons pear liqueur
  (Poire William)
1½ cups peeled, cored and chopped
  firm pears, such as Rocha or Bosc
1 teaspoon ground cinnamon
1 onion, finely chopped
scant 1 cup white wine

freshly ground black pepper
braised peas, roast potatoes, buttered
  carrots and a little finely grated
  orange zest, to serve

Caramelized pears:
2 tablespoons unsalted butter
2 small sweet, juicy pears, such as
  Rocha or Bosc, skin left on, cored
  and cut lengthwise into wedges
1 teaspoon raw brown sugar
2 tablespoons pear liqueur
  (Poire William)

Heat the oven to 325°F. Rub the kosher salt over the skin of the duck. Heat a large Dutch oven over high heat until very hot. Add the duck, skin side down, and fry 5 minutes, or until sealed and brown. Pour off the excess fat, then turn the duck over and brown the other side. Add the liqueur and bubble for a few minutes until it evaporates. Remove the duck from the pot and leave to one side.

Add the chopped pears to the remaining duck fat in the Dutch oven, sprinkle with the cinnamon and cook over medium heat 5 minutes, or until just golden. Add the onion and fry 5 minutes longer. Return the duck to the pan, season with salt and pepper and add the wine. Cover and cook 2 hours, or until the duck is tender and cooked through.

Just before the duck is ready, make the caramelized pears. Melt the butter in a skillet over medium-high heat. Add the pear wedges and cook 5 minutes, turning frequently, or until soft. Sprinkle with the sugar, and, when it melts, pour the liqueur over and leave to bubble a few minutes until the pears caramelize. Serve the duck with the pan juices, caramelized pears, braised peas, roast potatoes and buttered carrots, sprinkled with a little orange zest.

POUSSINS WITH SOUR CREAM

This was one of my grandmother Valentine's favorite dishes, which she always associated with the famous Russian Valentina. Cooked in this way, the poussins become deliciously tender and the creaminess of the whole dish makes it really comforting and luxurious on a cold winter's night. We were always served this dish with braised red cabbage spiced up with a little cinnamon.

Serves 4
Preparation time: 20 minutes
Cooking time: 45 minutes

4 oven-ready poussins
2½ cups sour cream, plus extra
  if needed
2 bay leaves

3 tablespoons unsalted butter
4 potatoes, peeled and cut into
  paper-thin slices
kosher salt and freshly ground
  black pepper
broiled polenta, to serve (optional)

Heat the oven to 350°F. Bring a large saucepan of water to a boil over high heat, then lower in the poussins and cook 5 minutes over medium heat. Drain well, then transfer the poussins to a deep baking dish.

Pour the sour cream over, add the bay leaves and season with salt and pepper. Cover with a lid or foil and bake 30 minutes, or until the poussins are tender, adding more cream if necessary.

Meanwhile, melt the butter in a large skillet over medium-high heat. Add the potatoes and fry, turning frequently, until golden and cooked through. Season with salt and pepper.

Remove the poussins from the oven and transfer them to a large platter, then add the cooked potatoes to the baking dish. Stir them into the cream and juices from the poussins, then return the birds to the dish. Bake 10 minutes longer, or until the juices from the poussins run clear when the thickest part of the meat is pierced with the tip of a sharp knife. Discard the bay leaves and serve with broiled polenta, if you like.

PLUM & ALMOND TART

In my Nonna's garden there grew the loveliest, tangiest little plums, called *susine* in the local dialect. They were perfect for this fruit tart, which I've always thought has a slightly Russian feel.

Serves 4
Preparation time: 35 minutes,
  plus 30 minutes chilling
Cooking time: 30 to 40 minutes

Piecrust:
1½ cups all-purpose flour, plus extra
  for rolling and dusting
7 tablespoons chilled unsalted butter,
  cubed, plus extra for greasing
4 tablespoons sour cream

Filling:
2½ tablespoons unsalted butter,
  softened

¼ cup superfine sugar, plus
  2 tablespoons for sprinkling
2 eggs, beaten
1 cup finely ground blanched
  almonds

Topping:
6 large, ripe plums, quartered
  and pitted
4 tablespoons slivered almonds
8 tablespoons plum jam
1 teaspoon fruit-flavored vodka or
  plain vodka, for sprinkling (optional)

First, make the piecrust dough. Sift the flour into a mixing bowl and rub in the butter with your fingertips until the mixture resembles fine bread crumbs. Stir in the sour cream and combine to form a soft dough. Wrap the dough in plastic wrap and chill 30 minutes.

Heat the oven to 400°F and lightly grease a cookie sheet with butter. To make the filling, cream together the butter and sugar in a mixing bowl until light and fluffy. Mix in the eggs, alternating with the ground almonds.

Roll out the dough on a lightly floured work surface into a 12-inch circle. Put it on the greased cookie sheet and spread the almond mixture over, leaving a 1½-inch border all the way around the edge. Top with the plums, then turn in the dough border to form a raised edge. Bake 30 to 40 minutes until the plums are tender and the pastry is light brown.

Meanwhile, put the almonds in a dry skillet over medium-low heat and toast a few minutes, tossing the pan occasionally, until just golden. Take out of the pan and leave to cool.

When the tart is baked, slide it onto a wire rack. Put the plum jam in a small pan and warm through, then press through a strainer into a bowl. Brush the jam over the top of the tart, then sprinkle with the vodka, if using, the extra sugar and the toasted almonds. Leave to cool.

Top: Grandpa Gerard Scott, second from left Rose,
middle, with some of their children and friends.
Above, from left: Grandpa Gerard, Leonora,
Paula, Howard, Rose, Peter and Gerard.

3. *Rose* AT CLARIDGE'S HAVING TEA

One rainy Wednesday afternoon in the spring of 1889, my paternal grandfather, Gerard Schoetel, found himself in the grand, pillared foyer of Claridge's hotel, in Mayfair, London. He had recently left Holland, unnerved by the political situation at that time in mainland Europe. Apparently, he had been a professor at the university in Delft, but had decided to come and seek his fortune in London. It is clear, from what happened that afternoon, he was unfamiliar with the rules of decorum that applied to polite society in Victorian England. Either that or he was so overcome upon first seeing my grandmother he simply forgot himself.

Rose Daniels, my Irish grandmother, was quietly standing in a corner, waiting for her sister Beatrice to come out of the powder room. The sisters had just treated themselves to a sumptuous tea in the hotel; Rose, it is said, was especially partial to warm buttered crumpets and cake, and Trixie loved the hotel's famous scones. The tantalizing aroma of freshly baked cakes and cookies wafted gently through the foyer, mingling with the perfume from the perfectly arranged vases of flowers. The discreet chink of china cups and the crisp white tablecloths scattered with crumbs indicated tea was still in full flow, with a small line of people waiting to be seated.

Seeing Rose standing alone in a corner, and with complete disregard to what anybody watching might have thought of his impudence, Gerard walked straight up to her and boldly asked her name. Rose was so taken aback that she found herself replying, "Trixie," which wasn't her name at all, but rather her sister Beatrice's family nickname. By some strange logic, in her bewilderment and confusion,

> **The tantalizing aroma of freshly baked cakes and cookies wafted gently through the foyer... tea was still in full flow.**

Rose thought that if she did not give this handsome foreign stranger her real name, she would somehow not be breaking the rules of polite society.

Mesmerized, their gloved fingertips barely touching, they exchanged a few more words before the real Trixie returned from the powder room.

Then, according to family lore, Gerard gave Rose his solemn promise: "I am going to marry you." Rose, flushed and trembling from the encounter, must nonetheless have managed to slip Gerard her address before a horrified Trixie dragged her outside to find a taxi. Or, perhaps, he simply set about finding her with what few clues he had.

Six months later, Rose climbed down the thick honeysuckle growing outside her bedroom window at the darkest hour of the night and eloped with her handsome Gerard. Her family never spoke to her again. I know little about her because she died a long time before I was born, and by the time I was old enough to ask about Rose there was barely anyone left who had known her. Rose's eldest daughter, my Aunt Leonora, remembered a little: she told me Rose had a magnificent bosom, large enough to create a flat shelf that was big enough to balance her teacup upon, and that Gerard was always madly possessive of her. Apparently, my grandmother was also a very good cook.

Gerard changed his Dutch last name to Scott, and their complicated, peripatetic married life began. Through their many adventures, which took them all over the world in Gerard's insatiable desire to chase fortune whenever and wherever it beckoned him, he always called Rose by the name Trixie. There were nine children born from their stormy relationship, conceived in places as far away as Argentina, Australia and Egypt. In faded photographs I have been shown, the family stands as a large group of smiling figures. But by the time they returned to live in England they had only five surviving children: Gerard, Leonora, Paula, Peter and Howard, my father.

My grandfather was fiercely passionate about being a British citizen, and wherever the family happened to be—whether it was opal mining in Australia or burning up with silver-mine fever in Argentina—he insisted all his children had to be born on British soil. As a result, Rose had to endure countless voyages back to England, often in the last stages of pregnancy. Family legend has it that she gave birth on the dockside at Southampton at least twice. One story I particularly like, as it reflects the love that bound them, describes how Gerard paid for Rose to travel back to their home country from some far-flung place only to realize, once she had gone, how much he was missing her. He set sail with the entire household, on a faster boat than hers, and was on the quayside to meet her when her ship docked, having squandered all their money in the process.

I can hardly remember my grandparents being talked about at all, although a slight whiff of scandal seemed to pursue their memory throughout my childhood. Gerard's appalling—and completely groundless—jealousy caused all kinds of tensions and much broken china. Apparently, things got most heated on Sundays when he would become absolutely convinced he had seen some man in church giving Rose the glad eye. He would be equally certain she had glanced back winsomely from under the brim of her hat and seethed with jealousy throughout the entire service, glaring at everyone; then, as soon as the pair had returned home, he would start shouting his wild accusations. My father and his siblings would cower at the table as their Sunday lunch was sent flying through the air. "What would you have for your Sunday lunch instead?" I asked my aunt, Leonora. "Bread and butter," she replied, her bitterness evident even sixty years later.

I find it amazing that Rose, my resilient grandmother, remains such a mystery to me. She gave me Irish blood by her birth (ironically, her only bit of Englishness was acquired as a result of her marrying a Dutchman who then became so thoroughly English), but she left so few stories for my family to hand down. She had even lost touch with her dearly loved sister Beatrice after her elopement.

The recipes that I associate my grandmother with are as unashamedly romantic as she obviously was, and are based around the gorgeous, girly afternoon tea on the day she fell in love.

From left my grandmother Rose and Grandpa Gerard with family and friends at a family christening.

LAVENDER SCONES

The unmistakable scent of lavender makes these scones very special. I find lavender somehow reminiscent of an era long gone. Be careful not to use too much when cooking, as it can completely overpower all other flavors and turn bitter. Rose Petal Jam (see page 40) is especially delicious with these scones.

Makes 12
Preparation time: 20 minutes,
   plus making the jam
Cooking time: 10 to 12 minutes

4 tablespoons chilled unsalted butter,
   cubed, plus extra for greasing
3 cups all-purpose flour, plus extra
   for dusting
1 tablespoon baking powder

2 tablespoons sugar
2 teaspoons fresh edible lavender
   or 1 teaspoon dried culinary
   lavender, coarsely ground
⅔ cup milk, plus extra for brushing
Rose Petal Jam (see page 40) and
   clotted cream or whipped cream,
   to serve

Heat the oven to 425°F and lightly grease a cookie sheet with butter. Sift the flour and baking powder into a mixing bowl. Add the butter and rub in with your fingertips until the mixture resembles fine bread crumbs.

In a separate bowl, combine the sugar and lavender, reserving a small amount of the mixture for sprinkling. Stir the mixture into the flour and butter, then add just enough of the milk to form a soft, sticky dough. Do not overwork the dough or the scones will be heavy.

Gently roll out the dough on a floured work surface until 1 inch thick. Using a sharp knife, cut out twelve 2-inch square scones (or use a 2-inch round cookie cutter dusted in flour). Don't pat down the edges of the scones, but leave the cut edges slightly rough, so the scones rise in layers as they bake.

Transfer the scones to the prepared cookie sheet, then brush the tops with a little milk and sprinkle with the reserved lavender sugar. Bake 10 to 12 minutes until risen and light golden brown. Slide onto a wire rack and leave to cool. Serve the scones with Rose Petal Jam and clotted cream.

LEMON & ELDERFLOWER CAKE

The delicate fragrance of elderflower is amazing when combined with lemon, and in this lovely teatime cake both flavor and scent come together beautifully.

Serves 8
Preparation time: 30 minutes
Cooking time: 30 to 35 minutes

Cake:
butter, for greasing
1 cup plus 2 tablespoons superfine
    sugar, plus 1 tablespoon for
    sprinkling
4 extra-large eggs
1⅔ cups all-purpose flour, sifted
2 tablespoons lemon juice
1 teaspoon finely grated unwaxed
    lemon zest

Glaze:
½ cup elderflower cordial
1 tablespoon finely grated unwaxed
    lemon zest
2 tablespoons sugar
2 edible elderflower heads, shaken
    and divided into small florets, plus
    edible flowers, to decorate

Filling:
1¼ cups heavy or whipping cream
2 tablespoons elderflower cordial

Heat the oven to 350°F. Line two shallow 8-inch cake pans with wax paper, then grease the paper with butter and sprinkle with the 1 tablespoon sugar. To make the cake, separate the eggs into 2 bowls, then cover and chill the egg whites. Whisk the yolks until fluffy, then sprinkle in the sugar, one spoonful at a time, and continue whisking until the mixture is thick, light and pale. Use a large metal spoon to gradually fold in the flour, alternating with the lemon juice and zest, until mixed together.

Whisk the egg whites until soft peaks form, then gently fold them into the flour mixture to make a batter. Divide the batter between the prepared pans and bake 20 to 25 minutes until golden and firm when lightly pressed with your finger. Leave to cool in the pans 5 minutes, then turn the cakes out onto a wire rack, remove the paper and leave to cool completely.

Meanwhile, make the glaze. Put the elderflower cordial, lemon zest and sugar in a small pan over low heat and heat, stirring until the sugar dissolves. Increase the heat slightly and boil 6 minutes, or until syrupy. Drop in the elderflower florets and remove from the heat. Leave to cool slightly, then strain through a fine strainer into a bowl.

To make the filling, whip the cream in a bowl until thick, then fold in the elderflower cordial. Spread the cream over one cake and top with the second cake. Lightly prick the top with a toothpick in several places, then spoon the warm glaze over and decorate with the flowers.

ROSE PETAL JAM

The roses with the most intense flavor are, not surprisingly, also the most intensely perfumed. This is a beautifully colored, fragrant jam that complements the Lavender Scones on page 36. Please do bear in mind any flowers intended for eating must be free of pesticides. Never eat or cook with flowers from florists, nurseries or garden centers, as in most cases these flowers will have been treated with pesticides.

Makes about 1 pound
Preparation time: about 30 minutes,
  plus overnight standing
Cooking time: about 30 minutes

8 ounces edible pink or red rose
  petals
2 cups sugar
juice of 2 lemons

Discard the bitter bottoms from the rose petals, snipping them off neatly with scissors. Gently rinse the petals under cold running water, then drain. Put them in a large, shallow bowl and sprinkle enough sugar over to coat each petal. Cover and leave to stand overnight.

The following day, put the remaining sugar, lemon juice and 4 cups water in a stainless-steel preserving pan or heavy-based saucepan over low heat and stir continuously to dissolve the sugar. Stir in the rose petals and simmer over very low heat 20 minutes.

Increase the heat to medium-high and bring to a boil, then boil hard 5 minutes, or until the mixture thickens and reaches 221°F on a candy thermometer, or a small spoonful of the mixture dropped onto a cold saucer and left to cool slightly sets and remains firm when pushed with your fingertip. Remove the pan from the heat and transfer the jam to a hot, dry sterilized jar and fill to within ¼ inch of the top. Seal immediately while the jam is still hot and then leave to cool. Store in a dark, cool place until required.

Cook's Note: To sterilize jam jars, wash them well, then keep immersed in boiling water until required. At home, we would quickly wipe the insides of the glass jars with a piece of cheesecloth dipped in pure alcohol just before adding the jam to guarantee they were completely clean and germ-free.

CUCUMBER SANDWICHES WITH A TWIST

I cannot help feeling Beatrice and Rose must have eaten cucumber sandwiches that afternoon at Claridge's, so I have added a recipe for them—my modern interpretation of this great teatime classic.

Serves 4
Preparation time: 15 minutes,
   plus 30 minutes standing

1 cucumber, peeled and sliced
   very thinly
½ teaspoon kosher salt
scant ½ cup parsley leaves
1 tablespoon olive oil

2 teaspoons lemon juice
3 tablespoons cream cheese
2 tablespoons pine nuts
8 slices of white bread
1½ ounces watercress, leaves
   picked off
¼ teaspoon paprika

Sprinkle the cucumber with the salt and leave in a colander to drain 30 minutes, then rinse and pat dry with paper towels.

Put the parsley, oil, lemon juice, cream cheese and pine nuts in a food processor and whiz until just smooth.

Thinly spread 4 slices of the bread with half of the cream cheese mixture. Top each with a layer of watercress leaves and then a layer of cucumber. Sprinkle very lightly with the paprika.

Spread the remaining slices of bread with the remaining cream cheese, put on top of the cucumber, spread-side down, and sandwich together. Cut off the crusts, slice into neat triangles or fingers and serve immediately with any remaining watercress.

My Nonna Valentine de Dudzeele.

4. LILI AND THE PRINCE OF *Montenegro*

In the late 1800s, my maternal grandmother, Valentine de Dudzeele, and her parents and siblings left their London house in Mayfair for a new diplomatic posting in Belgrade, where they were to take up their duties alongside the other embassy families. Soon after settling into their new home, they were invited to an official dinner and ball at the royal palace. The dinner was terminally long and formal. It featured many of Serbia's heavy, rich, meaty specialties: soup followed by several courses of broiled meat (served with typically spicy, hot Serbian sauces), cabbage leaves stuffed with nuts and the traditional *Beagradska torta od Badema* (Belgrade almond cake), all washed down with plenty of wine and *šljivovica*—the plum brandy that is still the national drink of the country. When the dinner had finally ended, the young King Alexander rose from the table unsteadily and requested a dance with Valentine.

Valentine, aware of the importance of never upsetting a king, smiled graciously and allowed him to lead her to the dance floor. She tried desperately to avoid Alexander stepping on her dancing feet, while he fumbled in his suit pockets for boiled sweets, sucking them throughout the waltz.

On the other side of the glittering ballroom, hung with chandeliers and lit by thousands of candles, Valentine's beloved younger brother, Bob, was dancing with the young Natalia Konstantinovic. She was unusually beautiful, with amazingly deep, expressive eyes of different colors: one brown, the other a deep emerald green flecked with gold. Her father, General Konstantinovic, watched them indulgently, safe in the knowledge that Natalia would soon marry Prince Mirko of Montenegro, as had long been planned.

> Valentine, aware of the importance of never upsetting a king, smiled graciously... and allowed him to lead her to the dancefloor.

Natalia and Bob fell deeply in love that night. They kept their love secret for a whole year. Under cover of the various theatrical and musical presentations given by the offspring of the diplomatic families, and organized by Valentine and her sister Germaine, Bob and Lili— as he always called Natalia—were able to meet often. But their secret happiness could not last. Lili's planned marriage was inevitable as it represented a significant political union. Despite Valentine and Germaine's valiant efforts to help, keeping the lovers out of sight of the various spies and conspirators that seemed to pepper their life, soon the suspicions of General Konstantinovic were aroused. He summoned a quaking young Bob to his house and ordered the boy to swear never to contact Natalia again and to forget her forever.

> **... filled with fear and despair at the thought of never seeing one another again, the young lovers met...**

Later that night, filled with fear and despair at the thought of never seeing one another again, the young lovers met in the gardens of the de Dudzeele house. Bob had brought a little picnic for them: a slice of Lili's favorite almond cake, a handful of cherries and a thick wedge of firm, white cheese. When the last cherry had been eaten, using Bob's carefully wiped penknife they sliced into their thumbs and pressed their wounds together to form a blood pact. Under the moon and stars they swore eternal love, no matter what might happen. Lili and Bob did not see each other again for a long time.

In 1895, the de Dudzeele family left Serbia for their next posting to Constantinople (where, five years later, Valentine was to meet my grandfather, Carlo Sforza). Lili married Prince Mirko, in Cetinje, on July 25, 1902, but it was not a happy time. The miserable girl wrote letter after letter to Queen Elena of Italy, Mirko's sister, begging her to free her from her marriage and obligations. She also wrote many letters to Valentine. Those she wrote in reply took months to reach her friend.

Queen Elena eventually arranged Lili's safe passage over the border into Italy. Lili took her young sons with her, traveling south to one of the royal palaces near Naples, where she took up temporary residence. As soon as Valentine heard that Lili and her sons had arrived safely, she traveled from Rome to stay with her. Lili's estranged husband made no attempt to contact her but the women both knew that she would never be able to marry Bob while Mirko still lived, such would be the scandal of their union. Lili, who was then only 26, resigned herself to having no contact with Bob.

Mirko died less than a year later in Vienna, and Valentine telegraphed Bob immediately. The telegram contained only two words: "Lili *libre*." He raced from Paris and they were married as soon as decorum would allow. Bob took his wife back to Paris, where they lived together for many happy years, just as they had promised each other they would do when they were barely more than children.

The recipes that follow are traditional dishes Lili would have grown up with and Valentine would have come to know during her stay in Belgrade. The dishes of these parts are derived from a mixture of other cuisines, mostly influenced by the Mediterranean, especially Greece and Turkey, but also Hungary and Austria. The former Yugoslavia has always had a passion for food, its people relishing the filling, meaty menus, enlivened by various sauces and condiments, and the *šljivovica* (plum brandy) and *lozovaca* (grappa) that accompany them. Traditionally, a Serbian menu has three courses: a soup, such as *pasulj*, the hearty white bean soup, with or without pork; followed by a stew or broiled meat; and a dessert, usually a cake. Lili, we know, was especially fond of the Belgrade almond cake with its sweet, buttery filling.

Uncle Bob, pictured far right, with family and friends.

CHICKEN PAPRIKASH

This is a Serbian recipe that we would often be served when visiting some of our cousins on Lili's side of the family. I always think you get the most flavor out of cooking chicken skin-on and bone-in, but this recipe also works with boneless, skinless chicken, and is slightly quicker to cook that way.

Serves 4
Preparation time: 10 minutes, plus 15 minutes standing
Cooking time: about 45 minutes

2 pounds 7 ounces chicken pieces, preferably thighs and legs
3 tablespoons unsalted butter
3 large onions, thinly sliced, top to root
2 tablespoons sweet paprika, preferably Hungarian
1 teaspoon hot paprika or cayenne pepper, plus extra for sprinkling
1 cup chicken stock
½ cup sour cream
kosher salt and freshly ground black pepper
boiled new potatoes and 1 tablespoon chopped parsley leaves, to serve

Put the chicken pieces in a colander and sprinkle all over with salt. Leave the chicken pieces to stand 15 minutes, then pat them dry with paper towels.

Heat the butter in a large frying pan with a tight-fitting lid over medium-high heat. Add the chicken, skin side down, and cook 4 to 5 minutes until brown, then turn over and cook 2 to 3 minutes longer. Remove from the pan and leave to one side.

Add the onions to the pan and cook 7 minutes, stirring occasionally and scraping up the brown bits from the bottom of the pan, or until light brown. Add both paprikas, season with pepper and stir to combine. Pour in the chicken stock, again scraping up the brown bits, then return the chicken pieces to the pan, on top of the onions.

Cover the pan and bring the liquid to a boil, then reduce the heat to low and simmer 20 to 25 minutes until the juices from the chicken run clear when the thickest part of the meat is pierced with the tip of a sharp knife.

Remove the pan from the heat, take out the chicken and keep warm. Leave the cooking juices to cool for a minute, then gradually stir the sour cream into the sauce and add a little more salt, if you like. If the sauce cools, return the pan to the heat to just warm through. Return the chicken to the pan and spoon the sauce over the top. Serve the chicken with new potatoes, sprinkled with parsley.

PORK, PAPRIKA & PEPPER CASSEROLE

This is a slow-cooked pork casserole with a good hint of paprika and a lovely sweetness from the peppers. While it is similar to a traditional goulash my ancestors were likely to have been served, I have finished this version off with crisp bacon and salty feta for extra zing, and served it with creamy polenta.

Serves 6
Preparation time: 20 minutes
Cooking time: 3½ hours

4 pounds lean boneless pork leg, trimmed of fat and cut into small cubes
4 tablespoons hot Hungarian paprika
1 tablespoon salt
1 teaspoon cayenne pepper
¼ cup firmly packed brown sugar
1 stick (½ cup) unsalted butter
14 ounces slab bacon, cut into ¼-inch strips

1 large Spanish onion, diced
2 red bell peppers, halved, seeded and diced
2 yellow bell peppers, halved, seeded and diced
1 garlic bulb, cloves finely minced
3½ cups chicken stock
3½ ounces feta cheese, crumbled
soft polenta or mashed potatoes, to serve

In a large bowl, toss together the pork pieces, paprika, salt, cayenne pepper and brown sugar until the meat is well coated, then leave to stand 5 minutes.

Meanwhile, melt the butter in a large frying pan with a tight-fitting lid over medium heat. Add the bacon and fry until crisp. Remove from the pan using a slotted spoon, and drain on paper towels.

Heat the fat remaining in the pan over medium-high heat. Working in small batches, add the pork cubes and fry until sealed and brown all over. Remove the pork from the pan using a slotted spoon and leave to one side. Repeat until all the meat is brown, then leave to one side. Discard any of the unused spice mix left in the bowl.

Add the onion to the pan over medium heat and fry gently until soft and translucent. Add the peppers and garlic and cook 4 minutes, or until soft.

Return the pork to the pan and pour in the chicken stock. Bring to a boil, then reduce the heat to low and simmer, covered, 3 hours, or until the pork is very tender. Scatter the feta and the crisp bacon over the pork, and serve with soft polenta.

STUFFED CABBAGE LEAVES

This is a really delicious way of serving Savoy cabbage and typical of the dishes Lili would have grown up with and the de Dudzeeles enjoyed during their time in Belgrade. It's very simple to make and a great vegetarian main course, with the ground walnuts adding a lovely flavor and texture to the whole dish.

Serves 4
Preparation time: 25 minutes,
  plus cooling
Cooking time: 1 hour 35 minutes

½ cup long-grain white rice
1 large Savoy or spring cabbage, left
  whole with hard core removed
1 cup walnuts
3 tablespoons olive oil

5 onions, roughly chopped
2 celery sticks, finely chopped
1 green bell pepper, halved, seeded
  and roughly chopped
1 can (15-oz.) plum tomatoes,
  drained, juice reserved and
  tomatoes chopped
kosher salt

Boil the rice in a pan of boiling salted water 10 to 15 minutes until tender. Drain and leave to cool before using.

Bring another large saucepan of salted water to a boil. Add the cabbage and return the water to a boil, then reduce the heat and simmer 5 to 6 minutes until soft. Meanwhile, grind the walnuts to fine crumbs using a mortar and pestle or food processor. Put the nuts in a bowl and leave to one side.

Drain the cabbage, refresh under cold running water and drain again. Leave to cool, then separate each leaf. Lay the larger leaves flat on a board. (You want 8 to 12 large leaves; the smaller leaves can be saved for another dish.)

Heat the oil in a skillet over medium heat. Add the onions, celery and green pepper and fry 5 minutes, or until soft. Add the cooked rice and stir-fry 2 minutes until the rice is thoroughly reheated. Remove the skillet from the heat, stir in the ground walnuts and season with salt.

Spoon about 1 tablespoon of the mixture onto a cabbage leaf. Roll up the leaf, with the sides folded inward to prevent the mixture from falling out. Repeat with the remaining leaves and mixture. Transfer the stuffed leaves to a large frying pan with a lid, making sure they fit snugly.

Spoon the tomatoes and reserved juice over the leaves, topping up with enough water to cover. Cover with a lid, then simmer over medium-low heat 1 hour, or until the leaves are very tender, adding extra water, if necessary. Serve warm or at room temperature.

BELGRADE ALMOND CAKE

I remember eating a cake like this one with my Belgian cousins as a child and being surprised even then by the unusual method used to make it. My mother had shown me how to cream the butter and sugar first, then add all the other ingredients, but this very rich, delicious cake is made very differently.

Serves 12
Preparation time: 30 minutes,
    plus cooling
Cooking time: about 50 minutes

Cake:
butter, for greasing
⅓ cup self-rising flour, sifted, plus
    extra for dusting
8 eggs, separated
½ cup plus 2 tablespoons superfine
    sugar
⅔ cup blanched almonds,
    finely chopped

Filling:
10 egg yolks
½ cup plus 2 tablespoons superfine
    sugar
1 tablespoon all-purpose flour
5 cups milk
1 vanilla bean, split lengthwise and
    seeds removed
3¼ sticks (1½ cups plus
    2 tablespoons) unsalted butter
toasted slivered almonds, to decorate

Heat the oven to 375°F. Grease a deep 11¼-inch cake pan with butter, then dust with flour and tap out any excess.

To make the cake, beat the egg yolks and sugar in a mixing bowl until pale, then add the chopped almonds. In a separate bowl, whisk the egg whites until stiff, then fold in the flour using a metal spoon. Fold the almond mixture into the egg white mixture, then pour into the prepared pan. Bake 45 minutes, or until a skewer inserted into the middle comes out clean. Turn the cake out of the pan and leave to cool on a wire rack. When cold, cut the cake horizontally into 3 layers with a very sharp, serrated knife.

To make the filling, beat the egg yolks and sugar in a heatproof bowl until light and fluffy, then add the flour and mix well. Stir in the milk and add the vanilla seeds. Put the bowl over a saucepan of simmering water and cook, stirring continuously, until the mixture is thick enough to coat the back of a spoon. Remove the bowl from the heat and stir until the custard is cool. In a separate bowl, beat the butter until light and fluffy, then beat it into the custard.

Spread the filling over the three layers of the cake and sandwich the layers together. Cover the outside of the cake with the remaining filling. Decorate with the toasted almonds and serve.

The de Oudzeeles.

5.   TURKISH DELIGHT—THE LOVE STORY OF *Valentine* AND CARLO

Nonno Carlo Sforza and Nonna Valentine de Dudzeele were my mother's parents, and this is their love story. Valentine's parents were in the Belgian diplomatic corps and distant cousins of the King of Belgium, so the family was always being posted off to various, often exotic, locations. In 1900, when the story begins, the de Dudzeeles had been stationed in Constantinople for five years.

The handsome, tall, charismatic Carlo Sforza, then about thirty years old, was just beginning his career as a diplomat. He was posted to Constantinople at the Italian embassy in 1900. Valentine and Carlo, like all the younger set of the diplomatic corps, were very much a part of the social whirl, so it was inevitable they should meet at the parties, banquets, picnics or the musical soirées organized for their collective entertainment and distraction. One summer's day, while boarding a gulet moored on the Bosphorus for a Turkish picnic on the water, Valentine slipped on the wooden jetty, crushing her foot badly against the heavy wooden hull of the boat. Carried home in agony, she was confined to the veranda of her home, where she lay for hours on a chaise-longue with her badly broken foot resting on a stool.

My mother told me she was sure this painful injury was engineered by Valentine, so her burgeoning friendship with Carlo would have the chance to develop further. On her veranda, Valentine and Carlo would have the perfect opportunity to get to know each other, away from everybody else. It would not have surprised me if Valentine had carried out such an act, although it impressed me greatly, as my Nonna's ability to remain courageous and clear-headed in any situation was her salvation many times over the years.

> Valentine and Carlo, like all the younger set of the diplomatic corps, were very much a part of the social whirl...

During her recovery, Carlo became Valentine's constant companion, often reading aloud to her, always respectful and decorous, and with a chaperone always within earshot. He would bring her boxes of almond sweetmeats, on which she would nibble while sipping endless cups of sweetened mint tea. (My Nonna had a very sweet tooth, and I remember that there was always a silver bowl of sweetmeats, such as Turkish delight studded with emerald green pistachios, at her home when I visited her as a child. Her lifelong passion for sticky, nutty confections was probably born in Turkey, where she would have had her pick of a vast range of sweets and honey-soaked pastries.)

In time, my grandparents pledged their love to one another and became engaged, in secret. Carlo left for Peking soon after. In her diary entry on the day of his departure, Valentine recorded: "I shall marry him, or nobody!"

The de Dudzeele family stayed on in Constantinople, but Valentine decided she was not going to mope, and that the cure for her aching heart would be to keep herself as busy as possible. As well as conducting various diplomatic duties her father gave her, she decided to help the Armenian women, who were being persecuted in the slow build-up to what was finally to become a bloodbath in April 1915, when the Ottoman government embarked upon the systematic decimation of its civilian Armenian population. By 1923, virtually the entire Armenian population of Anatolian Turkey had disappeared. When Valentine was living in Constantinople, at the turn of the twentieth century, massacres were occurring throughout the empire. Her letters home to Brussels during this period are filled with descriptions of the terrible fighting that raged around her. In one letter, Valentine vividly describes being in the besieged Belgian legation, while gunfire rained down on the house. Two of Valentine's best friends were Armenian: Sophie Markarion and her husband Gabriel. Realizing what was likely to happen to them, Valentine and her sister Germaine set about to save them. The sisters had a very deep wardrobe in their bedroom and persuaded Sophie and Gabriel to live in it while they worked out what to do. They were assisted in their mission by their friend, the novelist Pierre Loti, who was at that time *lieutenant de vaisseau* (first lieutenant) in the French navy's fleet in the Bosphorus.

For several days, Sophie and Gabriel sat and slept in two comfortable armchairs the sisters had dragged into the wardrobe. Nobody could risk the staff finding out, as they would most likely tell the girls' father what was happening. A few days later, the sisters had secured tickets to Paris. For the first and most dangerous part of the journey, Sophie and Gabriel were hidden under the sisters' wide, long skirts on the floor of their official horse-drawn carriage, before finally being smuggled out of the country to safety.

*The King and Queen of Belgium, seated back,
with their family and Nonno Carlo far right.*

Sophie remained a close friend of my grandmother—known to us all as Madame Markarion—and, after Valentine died, she stayed in touch with my mother for several years. The Markarions eventually settled in Paris, where Sophie made a simple living for herself, often making *Sirop d'Oranges* (Orange Cordial, see page 63) in the bidet of her bathroom.

The intrepid escapades of the de Dudzeele sisters, for which they often disguised themselves as men or dressed up in traditional Turkish peasant clothing, worried Carlo enormously. Through Valentine's letters to him, he learned how frequently the girls put themselves in danger. He begged Valentine to be careful, but, despite his pleas, her determination was unshakable and many Armenian women owed much to her courage.

> During the eleven years of their engagement, Valentine kept the secret of her decision to marry Carlo from everyone, except for her sister...

During the eleven years of their engagement, Valentine kept the secret of her decision to marry Carlo from everyone, except for her sister Germaine. Germaine always kept a very comprehensive diary and, along with all the other little details of their daily life, she recorded the details of her sister's romance with great care, writing in violet ink with a distinctive, looping hand.

Throughout those years, Carlo worked hard and traveled widely to further his career, determined not to marry Valentine until he was wealthy and successful enough to offer her what he considered to be a worthy future. Fortunately, this did not mean that they remained entirely separated over these years. Once the de Dudzeeles had left Constantinople, Valentine and Carlo had the opportunity to see each other at functions in various different countries, always in an official capacity as part of the diplomatic corps.

Carlo and Valentine kept their love alive by writing letters to each other and they were finally married in Vienna on March 4, 1911. Carlo's brothers refused to attend. Even though my Nonna's lineage was impeccable, they declared she was not a good financial catch. In their mind, the family had made sacrifices to help Carlo further his diplomatic career and they felt, by marrying Valentine, he was throwing these back in their faces. Germaine, however, loved Carlo dearly and thought he was a perfect match for her sister.

My grandparents' wedding took place in the cathedral of St. Stephen, in Vienna, the city where Valentine's father was then Belgian Minister for Austria. A very small sapphire and diamond brooch was sent as a wedding gift for the thirty-six-year-old bride from the Sforza family. Valentine's wedding dress was trimmed with lace she and Germaine had made together, dipping the strips of exquisitely delicate fabric in coffee to stain it to the right shade.

After a traditional Viennese meal of *rindsuppe* (meat soup), *topfen strudel* (cheese strudel) and *tafelspitz* (boiled beef with applesauce and horseradish), they cut into a beautiful Sacher torte that had been made for their wedding. (Many years later in Rome, my mother described her mother's wedding feast, as I practiced stretching the finest of strudel pastry, and furiously beating air into my eggs to create the perfect Sacher torte for my end-of-year chef exams.) After their honeymoon in Venice, the newlyweds, now Count and Countess Sforza, went on to Montignoso, Italy, to meet Giovanni, Carlo's father.

Giovanni, a widower, was a curmudgeonly, very serious man who had retired from his life in Turin to live in almost complete solitude on the ground floor of the immense Sforza family palace on the Via Aurelia. There he developed his passion as a local historian and wrote many books.

Valentine's meeting with her father-in-law was to remain etched in her memory forever, especially their first lunch together. They followed him meekly to the dining room, where the maid served several simple Tuscan dishes, which they ate in silence: bowls of boiled beans drizzled with home-pressed olive oil; plates of hand-sliced, home-cured ham with generous slices of homemade unsalted bread; and a thick soup, made using the vegetables grown in the small vegetable patch outside the kitchen door. This first lunch, as with the many other meals that the three of them shared over time, took place without conversation.

> They followed him meekly to the dining room where the maid served several simple Tuscan dishes, which they ate in silence.

My grandparents' long-awaited move to Peking, where Carlo was to take up his first posting as Italian ambassador, did not come a moment too soon. They finally set sail for China in May 1911.

SPICY CHICKEN WITH EGGPLANT CREAM

A little taste of Turkey—my mother used to cook this dish often and it would provoke my father to talk to us about his favorite book, *One Thousand and One Nights*.

Serves 4
Preparation time: 30 minutes,
   plus cooling and 20 minutes soaking
Cooking time: about 1 hour

2 large tomatoes
3 tablespoons unsalted butter
4 skinless, boneless chicken breast
   halves, cut into large cubes
4 small onions, roughly chopped
4 garlic cloves, thinly sliced
2 red bell peppers, seeded
   and chopped
1 teaspoon chili powder
2 cups chicken stock
kosher salt and freshly ground
   black pepper

Eggplant cream:
4½ pounds eggplants
juice of ½ lemon
1 tablespoon salt
3 tablespoons unsalted butter
3 tablespoons all-purpose flour
1¼ cups milk
4 tablespoons grated hard cheese,
   preferably Turkish, or Parmesan,
   Pecorino or Regato
2 tablespoons pomegranate seeds,
   paper-thin slices of lemon and
   2 tablespoons chopped parsley
   leaves, to serve

Heat the oven to 350°F. Cut a cross in the bottom of each tomato, using a sharp knife, then put them in a heatproof bowl and cover with boiling water. Leave to stand 2 to 3 minutes, then drain. Peel off and discard the skins, then roughly chop the flesh and leave to one side.

To make the eggplant cream, pierce the eggplants all over with a fork and put them on a roasting rack over a roasting pan. Roast 35 minutes, or until soft. Leave them to cool, then peel and cut off the tops. Pour 1¼ cups water into a bowl and stir in the lemon juice and salt. Add the eggplant pulp and soak 20 minutes, or until required.

To cook the spicy chicken, melt the butter in a large skillet with a tight-fitting lid over medium heat. Add the chicken and fry until light brown all over. Add the onions, garlic, red peppers, tomatoes, chili powder and stock and season with salt and pepper. Stir and bring to a boil. Reduce the heat, cover and simmer 20 minutes, or until the chicken is cooked through.

Drain the eggplants, then squeeze dry. Melt the butter in a large skillet, then stir in the flour until smooth. Add the eggplant pulp and mash into the butter paste with a fork. Gradually add the milk and whisk together, then stir in the cheese and simmer until thick. Serve the eggplant cream topped with the chicken, pomegranate seeds, lemon and parsley.

TURKISH BULGUR, POMEGRANATE & ALMOND SALAD

This is a gorgeous-to-look-at and simply scrumptious salad my mother would often make for us. It was always guaranteed to make her reminisce about her own mother's escapades in faraway Constantinople.

Serves 4 to 6
Preparation time: 20 minutes, plus cooling
Cooking time: 15 minutes

1 cup coarse bulgur wheat
14 ounces cherry tomatoes, halved
5 tablespoons slivered almonds
1 pomegranate
1 cup canned chickpeas, drained and rinsed

3 tablespoons roughly chopped mint leaves
grated zest of 1 unwaxed lemon
kosher salt

Dressing:
2 tablespoons pomegranate molasses
2 tablespoons lemon juice
3 tablespoons extra virgin olive oil
½ teaspoon dried chili flakes

Bring a large saucepan of water to a boil. Add the bulgur wheat and cook according to the package directions until tender. Drain and leave to cool.

Meanwhile, heat the broiler to medium. Put the cherry tomatoes on a baking tray and broil 8 to 10 minutes until soft, then transfer to a bowl and leave to cool. Scatter the almonds on the baking tray and broil a minute or two until light brown, checking frequently to make sure they don't burn. Leave to cool.

Roll the pomegranate on a flat work surface until the skin begins to loosen from the fruit. Cut it in half and then, over a bowl, remove the seeds from the membrane using a teaspoon. Remove any skin or pith and leave to one side.

Put the cooked bulgur, chickpeas, cherry tomatoes, almonds, 4 tablespoons of the pomegranate seeds, mint and lemon zest in a large serving bowl. Toss to combine and season with salt.

Mix together all the dressing ingredients in a small bowl and season with salt. Just before serving, pour the dressing over the salad and toss together well.

SEKERPARE

This very traditional Turkish sweetmeat might well have been the kind of thing my grandparents would have nibbled together at the start of their romance, when they were falling in love in Constantinople.

Serves 16
Preparation time: 30 minutes,
   plus 15 minutes resting and
   10 minutes standing
Cooking time: 40 minutes

2¼ sticks (1 cup plus 2 tablespoons)
   unsalted butter, softened
heaped 1 cup confectioners' sugar,
   sifted
2 egg yolks

1¼ cups fine semolina
1¾ cups all-purpose flour, sifted
1 teaspoon baking powder
16 blanched almonds
fresh mint tea, to serve

Syrup:
1¼ cups sugar
2 tablespoons lemon juice

To make the syrup, put the sugar, lemon juice and 2 cups water in a saucepan and bring to a boil. Boil 15 minutes, stirring occasionally, until thick and syrupy, then remove the pan from the heat and leave the syrup to cool.

Meanwhile, combine the butter and confectioners' sugar in a mixing bowl, add the egg yolks and mix well with your hands. Add the semolina, then mix in the flour and baking powder gradually (otherwise the mixture will clump together). Add a few drops of water if it looks dry and continue mixing until it comes together into a ball of dough. Continue to work the dough with your hands until it is very soft and pale. Wrap the dough in plastic wrap and leave to rest 15 minutes.

Heat the oven to 315°F and line a cookie sheet with wax paper. Shape the dough into 16 equal, small balls and put them on the prepared cookie sheet. Lightly press the top of each piece to flatten slightly and push an almond into the middle.

Bake 20 to 25 minutes until light golden brown. Remove the pastries from the cookie sheet with a spatula and place on a wire rack to cool slightly, then transfer to a shallow baking pan.

Gently reheat the syrup, then, using a tablespoon, spoon the warm syrup over the pastries. Repeat a few times so a puddle of syrup forms in the pan, then leave the pastries to sit in the syrup about 10 minutes to soak it up. Remove the pastries from the syrup, arrange on a plate and serve with fresh mint tea.

SOPHIE'S ORANGE CORDIAL

I always make this in memory of Madame Markarion and my Nonna's amazing courage. It is really refreshing on a hot summer's day, diluted with water and served over ice. Decorate with a sprig or two of fresh mint before serving.

Makes about 4 cups
Preparation time: 20 minutes,
  plus cooling
Cooking time: 1 hour

grated zest of 2 large unwaxed
  oranges

4½ cups freshly squeezed orange juice
6 cups sugar

Mix the orange juice and sugar together thoroughly in a large saucepan, then stir in the orange zest.

Heat gently over low heat 1 hour, stirring continuously until the sugar dissolves and the mixture thickens. Do not allow to boil.

Leave to cool completely, then pour into sterilized glass bottles (see *Cook's Note*, page 40) and seal tightly with the caps. Once sealed, the cordial will keep up to 4 months until opened.

Nonna Valentine, middle, and Nonno Carlo, second from right, with friends on an informal outing in the Chinese countryside.

6. *Fiammetta* NEVER GOT THE HANG OF USING CHOPSTICKS

Carlo and Valentine, my maternal grandparents, arrived in Peking on June 24, 1911. It had been a long and rather dull month at sea, scarcely enlivened by the stiff meals of rather plain food at the captain's table. On docking, they were instantly engulfed by the many exotic sights, tastes and smells of China. It took them a little time to get used to and appreciate the new flavors they were offered: fresh ginger, star anise, fermented, salty sauces and the ever-present steamed or boiled rice. In China, my Nonna developed a lifelong preference for Lapsang Souchong tea, and its smoky aroma never fails to remind me of her.

My grandparents were to witness, often at first hand, a period of great unrest — punctuated by violence and war—as China struggled through a very difficult period in its history. The empire was disintegrating after the overthrow of the Manchu dynasty in 1911. For more than 2,000 years, China's government had centered on a monarchy; now, for the first time, the country was without an emperor. Her imperialist glory days were behind her—and China was a nation in decline, heavily controlled by foreign powers.

Peking had many European residents in the early 1900s, whose lifestyle could not have been more different to that of the Chinese citizens. The Europeans attempted to continue their routines and habits as though they were still at home, and they effectively treated the locals as their slaves. In hindsight, it was not surprising the Boxer Rebellion of 1900, which took place in the north and was ignited by anti-imperialist feeling, had found so many supporters in Peking.

A decade later, when Valentine and Carlo arrived in China, ripples from that nationalist uprising were still being felt. The foreign diplomats and their consorts, who welcomed Valentine and Carlo upon their arrival, lived in abject terror of the horrors of the rebellion happening all over again. My Nonna Valentine, over Lapsang Souchong tea and rather solid Chinese buns with the other legation wives, heard all about the famous German

> My grandparents were to witness, often at first hand, a period of great unrest—punctuated by violence and war—as China struggled...

Baron von Ketteler, who had been dragged from his sedan chair and brutally murdered at the start of the uprising.

Carlo and Valentine's official residence was in the legation, situated close to the other diplomatic homes, which encouraged neighborliness and a much-needed sense of unity and safety in numbers. Carlo had been posted to China before and was far better equipped to adjust to the dramatic differences in culture and the constant sense of danger and instability that surrounded them. Despite the problems, he always loved China, feeling the lure of the country most deeply, and he returned twice more in the course of his career, bringing back many beautiful items, many of which were passed on to me.

My Nonna would tell me how Carlo would delight in causing scandal among some of their more toffee-nosed neighbors. When it was hot he would love to pace around the veranda and garden wearing only his beautiful, bright-red silk kimono, which exposed rather more of his body than they wished to see. The neighbors' servants would arrive periodically on the doorstep to deliver stiffly worded, handwritten notes expressing their mistresses' complaints, to which Carlo took enormous pleasure in replying with the words: "Madam, if you do not wish to see, simply do not look!" He would then position himself deliberately where he could best be seen from every one of the adjacent houses, reading a book calmly in the sunshine.

Carlo discovered that, in Valentine, he had the best ally and confidante. She had a strong sense of the ridiculous, coupled with an amazing ability to rise above both her disgust and fear, which cannot have been easy in China during that time. Many years later, when I would visit her for tea after school in Rome, she would tell me the story of how she would hide inside the Italian legation, peeping through the branches of the mimosa tree planted beneath her window, watching the latest riot unfolding in the street below. She would describe calmly, between bites of chocolate cake, how there were many casualties and that the fighting often raged for hours.

It was Valentine's responsibility, in the midst of all this ugliness outside the legation, to behave like an ambassadress, entertaining regularly—conventions she had learned only too well through the long years of supporting her father in his various diplomatic postings around the world. One of the most memorable events for her was when the three princesses from the Manchu dynasty came to an official dinner. Valentine had tried very hard with the menu, attempting a meal that at least leaned toward being Italian, even though

My mother, Fiammetta, with Nonno Carlo.

so many ingredients were not available. She tried, unsuccessfully I am told, to get the cook to create some kind of a pasta dish using Chinese noodles and tomatoes. Try as she might, though, it was too difficult to persuade the cook to limit the hot, spicy quality of many of the dishes and the seemingly endless number of them served.

As it turned out, Valentine need not have worried about trying to make the meal taste authentic or be in any way representative of Italian food. As far as the princesses were concerned, anything they did not like to eat or drink could simply be tossed over their shoulders onto the floor. And anyway, the food was not half as interesting as the toilet: they spent half the evening flushing it and shrieking with laughter as they watched the water gurgle away. Flushing toilets were something of a rarity in China in those days—they were a novelty, even for royalty.

> **As far as the princesses were concerned, anything they did not like to eat... could simply be tossed over their shoulder...**

On October 3, 1914, at the age of 39, Valentine gave birth in her home in Peking to Fiammetta, my mother. War had broken out in Europe and the time was fast approaching when Carlo and Valentine would have to return home. Most of the British nannies in Peking had already gone back to take up their nursing careers in their war-torn homeland, so Valentine hired a *tama* (a Japanese nurse) to care for Fiammetta. (The other ladies in the diplomatic corps reliably informed her they were considerably cleaner than the Chinese nurses, who had a tendency not to wash very often.)

The following year, the family sailed on to their next posting in Belgrade, only to discover in the course of the long voyage that all the diplomatic families had already been evacuated to Corfu, where their ship was duly diverted. They spent a few worrying years on the Greek island, wondering what would happen. Valentine tried to keep calm for the sake of her two-year-old daughter and her baby son, Sforzino, but it was hard. She and Carlo heard some blood-curdling tales about what was going on in mainland Europe from the various retreating Yugoslavian soldiers who appeared sporadically on the island.

Carlo was fast becoming a recognized and respected political voice, and the family was recalled to Rome in June 1919. The following year, Carlo was elected senator to the Kingdom of Italy, and the family moved into the ministerial residential building of La Consulta, situated opposite the Palazzo del Quirinale, where Carlo was to work. Both children began their formal education at the original Maria Montessori School.

Many years later, as a little girl, when I visited my grandmother in her Rome apartment, I always felt awed by her amazing collection of Chinese antiques and memorabilia. If I was very good, I would be allowed to play very carefully with some of the pieces. Only now, on reading Nonna's letters and looking through her photographs, do I really appreciate what an incredible woman she was to have come through so many turbulent experiences unscathed.

Carlo never took to Chinese food, but my Nonna passed down her love of it to my mother, and through her to me. Whenever my father took us to our favorite Chinese restaurant in Soho, London, however, I was always disappointed my mother did not know how to use chopsticks, despite spending time in the Far East. With the logic of a child, I had always presumed she would handle them like a native.

Above, my mother with her Japanese tama.
Left Carlo and Valentine, pictured far left

CHINESE TEA-SMOKED DUCK

As a tribute to my grandmother's love of Lapsang Souchong tea, I have used it as the base of the smoking mixture in this recipe. Whenever my mother and I prepared this together, we made sure all the kitchen windows were open, as the aroma of the smoking tea is all-pervasive and persistent.

Serves 4
Preparation time: about 20 minutes, plus 15 minutes resting
Cooking time: about 1 hour 15 minutes

4½-pound whole prepared duck, excess fat removed
½ cup soy sauce

2 star anise
1 cinnamon stick
½ cup long-grain white rice
¼ cup Lapsang Souchong tea leaves
½ cup sugar
shredded Chinese cabbage, cucumber batons, chopped scallions and steamed rice (optional), to serve

Rinse the duck thoroughly with boiling water, then pat dry with paper towels. Lightly prick the skin all over with a skewer or thin-bladed knife, but do not pierce the meat.

Put three-quarters of the soy sauce, the star anise, cinnamon stick and ½ cup water in the bottom of a large steamer. Alternatively, use a large saucepan fitted with a wire rack. Put the duck in the steamer basket or on the rack, cover and steam, topping up with extra boiling water if necessary, 45 minutes, or until the duck is cooked through and the juices run clear when a thigh is pricked with a sharp knife. Reserve 6 tablespoons of the pan juices.

Line a large wok or heavy-based roasting pan with thick aluminum foil. Mix together the rice, tea and sugar and add to the wok. Fit a wire or roasting rack on top so it is about 1 inch above the rice mixture. Put the duck, breast side up, on the rack, then cover with a double layer of foil and/or a lid—the covering should be at least 1 inch above the top of the duck. Make sure there are not any gaps around the edge of the wok or pan.

Put the wok or pan over high heat. When the mixture begins to smoke (try to patch up any gaps in the foil) cook 10 minutes, then reduce the heat to medium and smoke 15 minutes longer. Turn the heat off and leave to rest, covered, 15 minutes. Remove the duck from the wok or pan and discard the smoking mixture and foil. Carve the duck and serve on top of a bed of Chinese cabbage, cucumber and scallions. Heat the reserved pan juices with the remaining soy sauce and spoon it over the duck. Serve with rice, if liked.

PORK TENDERLOIN IN A PEKING STYLE

This is not an authentic Chinese recipe, of course, but it was a great favorite of my Nonna's. I like to prepare the greens with an Italian twist, using a combination of bok choy and savoy cabbage or cavolo nero.

Serves 4
Preparation time: 30 minutes,
 plus 1 hour marinating
Cooking time: 40 minutes

2¼ pounds pork tenderloin, trimmed
 of fat
6 tablespoons honey
4 teaspoons sesame seeds
3 to 4 tablespoons olive oil, plus extra
 for greasing
3 garlic cloves, finely chopped
1 to 2 teaspoons dried chili flakes
5 ounces shiitake mushrooms,
 halved
2 bok choy, quartered lengthwise

8 large savoy cabbage or cavolo nero
 leaves, shredded
kosher salt and freshly ground
 black pepper
steamed brown or white rice, to serve
 (optional)

Marinade:
6 tablespoons dark soy sauce
3 tablespoons sunflower or vegetable
 oil
3 garlic cloves, crushed
2½-inch piece gingerroot, grated
1 hot chili, seeded if you like and
 finely chopped

Mix together the marinade ingredients in a large, shallow, nonmetallic dish. Remove 2 tablespoons of the marinade and leave to one side. Put the pork in the remaining marinade and turn it to make sure it is well coated. Cover and marinate in the refrigerator 1 hour.

Heat the oven to 375°F. Remove the pork from the marinade and gently pat dry with paper towels. Discard the marinade. Brush the pork all over with the honey. Put the sesame seeds in a plate, then roll the tenderloin in the sesame seeds until well coated. Transfer the pork to a lightly greased rack over a roasting pan. Roast 25 to 30 minutes, turning occasionally, or until cooked through. Leave to rest 5 minutes.

While the pork is resting, heat a large wok or skillet over high heat. Add the oil and stir-fry the garlic and chili 30 seconds, without letting the garlic color. Add the mushrooms, bok choy and cabbage and toss together, turning them in the flavored oil until well coated. Add the reserved marinade and scant ½ cup water, then season with salt and pepper and stir-fry 5 minutes, or until the mushrooms, bok choy and cabbage are tender. Slice the pork and serve with the vegetable stir-fry and rice, if liked.

ORIENTAL-STYLE SCALLOPS

My mother and I devised this recipe together. I would have loved to cook it for my Nonna if she were still here to enjoy it with me.

Serves 6
Preparation time: 15 minutes
Cooking time: 10 minutes

2 tablespoons vegetable oil
7 ounces small broccoli florets
1 onion, thinly sliced
1 cup thinly sliced bok choy
5 ounces snow peas
2 cups sliced shiitake mushrooms

2 garlic cloves, finely chopped
2 teaspoons ground star anise
¼ teaspoon ground coriander
1 pound large sea scallops,
  roes removed
½ cup chicken stock
4 tablespoons rice wine vinegar
2 to 3 teaspoons soy sauce
steamed rice or egg noodles, to serve

Heat a large wok or skillet over high heat until very hot. Add the oil, broccoli and onion and stir-fry 3 to 4 minutes.

Add the bok choy, mushrooms, garlic, star anise and coriander and continue stir-frying 2 to 3 minutes longer.

Add the scallops, chicken stock, vinegar and soy sauce. Bring to a boil, then reduce the heat and simmer, uncovered, 3 minutes, or until the scallops are just cooked through and the vegetables are tender. Serve immediately with rice or noodles.

LYCHEE SORBET

My mother always told me I inherited my passion for this mysterious-tasting fruit from both her and my grandmother. This recipe makes a delicately flavored sorbet, which is ideal to serve at the end of several rich courses. I like to sprinkle it with edible flowers, such as the palest pink rose petals, and serve with a couple of fresh whole lychees in a martini glass.

Serves 6
Preparation time: 20 minutes,
  plus cooling and 4 hours freezing

30 ripe lychees, peeled and pitted
1 envelope (¼-oz.) unflavored gelatin
½ cup confectioners' sugar
1 teaspoon lemon juice

Using the back of a large metal spoon, squash the lychees in a strainer over a bowl and squeeze out the juice. Discard the lychee pulp.

Pour 2 cups plus 2 tablespoons just-boiled water into a heatproof bowl, sprinkle the gelatin over and leave to stand 5 minutes. Add the sugar, mixing well, then leave to cool.

Once cooled, strain the mixture through a fine strainer into a clean bowl. Stir in the lychee juice and lemon juice. Pour into a plastic container, cover and freeze 4 hours, or until solid, stirring every 30 minutes for the first 2 to 3 hours to prevent ice crystals forming. Alternatively, churn in an ice-cream machine according to the manufacturer's directions.

Once the sorbet is solid but not hard, spoon into martini glasses or pretty glass bowls to serve. If not using immediately, the sorbet can be frozen up to 1 month.

From left: Fiammetta, Nanny Mischa
and Sforzino.

7. FASCISM AND PARISIAN CUISINE WITH *Carlo*

The grand, airy top-floor apartment of the ministerial residence in Rome, La Consulta, was one of the most luxurious homes in which the family had ever lived. It was such a relief to have a settled home in Italy after their recent experiences in Constantinople, Peking and Corfu. Now, my grandfather, Carlo, was able to stroll across the cobblestoned piazza, past the splashing fountain and into the Quirinale, the Italian government building, where the view from the terraces is still one of the most impressive Rome has to offer. My mother and her brother settled into a happy routine under the ever-watchful eye of their Irish nanny, Mischa, while Valentine eagerly caught up with family and friends. Yet this period of calm was not to last.

It was the early 1920s, a decade known in Italy as *"gli anni ruggenti,"* a dynamic period of growth and advancement that was bound to bring about great social change. There were modern developments, such as the explosion of jazz music, Art Deco and a burgeoning feminist movement that brought about great changes in fashion and behavior in all Italian women. It was typified by the famous Italian tomboy flappers known as *maschiette*: young women of any social class who dressed and behaved in a manner uninhibited by tradition and considered shocking by their elders. Newly independent, unchaperoned and uncorseted Italian women emerged. No longer fragile flowers like their mothers and grandmothers, in the 1920s they became adventurous and daring. They raced cars, flew airplanes, wore makeup, smoked and drank. All of it fueled by innovations such as radio broadcasting, the phonograph and the cinema, and novelties like the creation of cocktails, including the famous Negroni.

> ... the explosion of jazz music, Art Deco and a burgeoning feminist movement brought about great changes...

But Italy's rejoicing over the end of World War I and a return to political normality was to be short-lived. A seemingly unstoppable wave of dark pessimism began to tighten its grip around the country and it made Carlo's job, and that of the entire Cabinet, very difficult. Taxes were high, wages low. The cost of living was exorbitant and there was a shortage of food, consumer goods and functioning public amenities. Riots, strikes, pilfering and violence began to increase throughout Italy, and behind the troubles Mussolini's voice was becoming increasingly powerful. Steadily, Mussolini's ideas for dramatic change found more and more fertile ground on which to grow, and support for him spread in a general atmosphere of deep-felt frustration and discontent. He seemed to offer the people of Italy order, discipline and progress in a time of great chaos and misery.

Carlo worked hard at the Quirinale, convinced from the very beginning that Italy under Mussolini would lose more than it would gain. Despite the support of Valentine, who was always ready to discuss anything with him, he felt increasingly isolated. When, in November 1919, Mussolini officially formed the Fascist Movement and joined the rest of the government in the Quirinale, Carlo watched with unease. Mussolini, though powerful, stood against all the beliefs that he and Valentine held so dear: freedom of expression, democracy and, above all, human dignity. Carlo was determined that the only way forward was to restore order through democracy and education, and repeatedly and fearlessly expressed his beliefs in his political speeches, newspaper articles, letters and books. Each time that he did, there was some form of violent reprisal. Most of Carlo's colleagues seemed to think everything would soon "blow over" and, despite his efforts, he found it increasingly difficult to persuade the king to understand his views or heed his warnings.

Valentine understood completely Carlo's position and shared his every fear and concern, so it was with profound relief and few regrets she packed up their lovely Consulta apartment to take her place alongside Carlo when he was elected ambassador to Paris on January 29, 1922. Their ambassadorial residence in Paris was a large, gray building with a big garden on the Rue de Varennes. Fiammetta and Sforzino, aged eight and six, were educated at home by a French governess, but still cared for by Nanny Mischa.

Valentine threw herself wholeheartedly into her glamorous role as the Italian ambassadress. Her favorite Parisian designers were Molyneaux and Beer, who created some fabulous gowns for her. My mother told me how Valentine would come up to kiss her goodnight before going out to

Top: the Sforza morning room
at La Consulta.
Left: Nonno Carlo with Sforzino
and Fiammetta on the beach.

a party, and she remembered one evening in particular, when her mother wore a beautiful low-waisted, pale-gray dress with a sparkling tiara in her hair.

Waiters, valets and butlers, wearing black knickerbockers and long white socks, staffed the house. There were glorious parties held in the large, elegant reception rooms. There were always after-dinner entertainments provided and sometimes Valentine would organize a performance by the well-known dancer, Loie Fuller, who would dance in the style of Isadora Duncan with much waving of chiffon scarves.

... Parisian cooking at this time was at its peak and highly respected internationally, it offered plenty of luxuries...

Fiammetta and Sforzino would watch from the garden, their noses pressed up against the glass of the window.

Valentine spent those nine months in Paris in a whirl of exhibitions, dinners, theater outings and gaiety. She also got involved in charity work, organizing the care of impoverished Italians living in Paris and trying to resolve the families' day-to-day difficulties. She hoped so much Carlo might put some of the current problems in Italy behind him for a while. Her role had always been one of support for her husband, but in Paris she thought they might enjoy themselves a little, too. They both loved good food and, as Parisian cooking at this time was at its peak and highly respected internationally, it offered plenty of luxuries and indulgences, such as ripe cheeses, pâtés, fresh oysters, delicate pastries, silky smooth sauces and the elusive pleasures of my Nonna's favorite feather-light soufflés.

Yet, for all this, it was impossible to ignore what was going on in Italy. Mussolini's voice, as Carlo had so accurately predicted, was growing louder and more powerful as more and more Italians heeded his words. The culmination came in October 1922, when Mussolini organized the March on Rome and took control of Italy. Carlo felt completely unable, morally or politically, to represent his country while it was governed by Mussolini and he resigned from his post as ambassador immediately. His friends and political colleagues tried to urge him to stay on, but Carlo, quite rightly, felt the situation would get much worse before it got any better.

Once Mussolini came to power, his policies and ideas affected every detail of people's lives, even the food they ate. For instance, the Battle of Wheat was established to boost cereal production to make Italy self-sufficient in grain, reduce the balance of trade deficit, lower the necessity for foreign imports of bread and, most of all, to show Italy off as a major force. Land that was often more suitable for growing other crops, such as olives and fruit, was taken over indiscriminately for the production of wheat. Mussolini ordered loaves of bread should have the word "Dux" (meaning "leader") molded or branded into the crust to farther underline his much publicized philosophy: bread is a symbol of simple Italian family life. Bizarrely, although in time there was a surfeit of wheat in Italy, pasta was declared by Mussolini as being "non virile," so it was left off the approved menu.

Carlo returned to Italy as a senator, hoping to take up his fight against Fascism from within his own country, at the Quirinale. Meanwhile, the family, with Nanny Mischa, took up temporary residence with the Sforzas at the Sforza Palace, in Montignoso, while they looked for a suitable home in Rome. Carlo often commuted back and forth, a journey that took almost a day.

In the little village of Montignoso, perched on the lower slopes of the Apuan Alps, just a few miles inland from the pretty Versilian coast, Valentine also had to contend with her in-laws. They had always deemed her unworthy of Carlo and were invariably cold and unwelcoming toward her. Determined to have a role in the house, and with Carlo away for long periods in Rome, Valentine took control as mistress of the household. She began with the kitchen, an area where she felt most confident, having had years of experience overseeing the various cooks in the many ambassadorial residences where the family had stayed, and where she had run all matters relating to the domestic arrangements.

Carlo returned to Italy as a senator, hoping to take up his fight against Fascism from within his own country...

Situated conveniently close to the back door of the kitchen was the huge wood-fired stove. Here, once a week, all the bread required by the household would be baked in one go. The bread dough would be placed in the *madia*, a kind of wooden trunk, to rise overnight on Tuesdays. Each Wednesday morning the loaves would be shaped and transported to the oven to be baked.

Valentine, being Belgian, did not like the unsalted Tuscan bread that the household was used to eating. She insisted at least a part of the dough should have salt added to it, and that this bread should be baked separately. So every week two loaves would appear, marked with a "V" for Valentine, for her exclusive pleasure. It was a small victory, but a precious one nevertheless, given the austere household rules imposed by her father-in-law.

Valentine was also adamant fresh coffee should be provided, and she gave the job of toasting and handgrinding the coffee to the housemaid, Maria. My mother would tell me how Maria would stand for hours, steadily turning the handle of the coffee-bean toaster—*la parchetta*—in front of the kitchen fire, her face growing red from the heat, while the whole house filled with the gorgeous aroma of freshly toasted coffee beans.

> So every week two loaves would appear, marked with a "V" for Valentine, for her exclusive pleasure. It was a small victory.

Valentine spent hours in the kitchen at Montignoso, teaching the cook to make a few new dishes, and introducing some lighter recipes to her standard repertoire of thick soups and stews. She encouraged the planting of a more varied selection of vegetables in the vegetable patch. One of the dishes with which she impressed everybody was the famous *galantina di pollo*, her own very complicated version of Galantine of Chicken (see page 84), as well as her delicious *turbante di riso ai gamberi* (rice ring mold with shrimp), which was served on special occasions and remains one of my favorite dishes.

Attempts at her much-loved soufflés were rather less successful in the kitchen's somewhat rudimentary wood-fired oven, especially as Maria would never heed my Nonna's warning: "Don't open the oven door yet, or it will collapse!" However, Nonna's Cherry Clafoutis (see page 89) always turned out beautifully, and my mother told me that she would look forward to the fruity dessert, made with the cherries from the tree growing in the garden. It was the children's favorite treat.

The family stayed at Montignoso until the spring of 1923 when they moved into their house on Via Linneo, in Rome. Unquestionably, Valentine did manage to change a few things during her stay and certainly made her mark in the kitchen, earning a little grudging respect from her father-in-law.

UNSALTED TUSCAN BREAD

Here is the original recipe from Montignoso for making the household bread, which I found among my Nonna's papers. It is the perfect base for so many of Tuscany's most classic dishes like *Pappa al Pomodoro* (Bread & Tomato Soup, see page 136) or ribollita (a twice-cooked bread and vegetable soup). If you prefer, add 1 teaspoon of fine kosher salt to the dough when you add the fermented starter to the flour, although for it to be truly authentic you should avoid adding salt.

Makes 1 large loaf
Preparation time: about 30 minutes,
   plus at least 4 hours fermenting and
   4 hours rising
Cooking time: 40 minutes

1 ounce fresh yeast, crumbled
3½ cups white bread flour or spelt
   flour, sifted, plus extra for dusting

Mix together the yeast, 3 tablespoons warm water and 1 teaspoon of the flour in a small bowl and cover with a folded, clean dish towel. Leave to ferment in a warm place about 4 hours, or preferably overnight.

Put the remaining flour in a large bowl and mix in the fermented starter and 3 tablespoons warm water to form a soft but not sticky dough (you might not need all of the water). Turn the dough out onto a floured work surface and knead 15 minutes, then transfer to a clean bowl, cover with plastic wrap and leave to rise in a warm, draft-free place at least 3 hours.

When the dough has risen, punch it down on a floured work surface and shape into a round loaf. Put the loaf onto a floured cookie sheet, cover with a lightly floured, clean dish towel and leave to rise 1 hour.

Heat the oven to 350°F. When the loaf has risen, bake 40 minutes, or until it sounds hollow when tapped on the base. Transfer to a wire rack to cool.

THE CONTESSA'S GALANTINE OF CHICKEN

My Nonna Valentine's *galantina di pollo* is still famous in the small Italian village of Montignoso. When I was a little girl, she usually served it cold, surrounded by a fascinating garnish of chopped aspic. Ask your butcher to bone the chicken for you.

Serves 6
Preparation time: about 30 minutes, plus 10 minutes resting
Cooking time: 1½ hours

14 ounces ground chicken, preferably leg and thigh meat
2 tablespoons tomato paste
2 tablespoons pistachio nuts, halved if large
4 tablespoons finely chopped herbs, such as parsley, chives, thyme and sage

1 chicken, about 3¼ pounds, boned
3 tablespoons roughly chopped dried apricots
9 ounces thick sliced Italian ham (*prosciutto cotto*), cut into ½-inch strips
3 tablespoons olive oil
kosher salt and freshly ground black pepper
green beans and boiled new potatoes, to serve

Heat the oven to 400°F. Put the ground chicken, tomato paste, pistachios and mixed herbs in a bowl and season with salt and pepper. Mix together until combined.

Lay the boned chicken, skin side down, on a clean cutting board. Spread half the filling mixture over the middle of the chicken. Scatter the apricots over, then lay the ham lengthwise down the middle. Finish with the remaining filling. Bring the sides of the chicken together, sealing in the filling. Reshape the chicken into a cylindrical shape and use a long skewer to secure the flesh together, or sew it closed with kitchen string.

Put the galantine in a roasting pan, breast side up. Coat it lightly with the oil and season with salt and pepper, then put it on the middle shelf of the oven and roast 20 minutes. Reduce the temperature to 350°F and cook 20 minutes longer.

Remove the chicken from the oven and turn it over, then roast 40 minutes longer. Remove the chicken from the oven again, turn it breast side up and roast 10 minutes longer until the juices from the chicken run clear when the meat is pierced with the tip of a sharp knife. If the chicken skin is still very pale, increase the temperature to 400°F for the final 10 minutes. Leave it to rest 10 minutes. Carefully remove the skewer or string, carve the chicken into neat slices and serve hot or cold with green beans and new potatoes.

MY GRANDMOTHER'S CHEESE SOUFFLÉ

We always made this for Nonna when she came to supper, as it remained her favorite long after she had left Paris. The secret, my mother would say, to a perfect soufflé is to make sure everyone is sitting at the dining table before it comes out of the oven. That way it can be whisked to the table before it has a chance to collapse! This recipe makes one large soufflé, but to make individual ones use four 1¼-cup ramekins and bake 20 minutes. You can serve the soufflé as a light main course with a green salad, or as an appetizer.

Serves 4
Preparation time: 25 minutes
Cooking time: 55 minutes

2 tablespoons unsalted butter, softened, plus extra for greasing
5 teaspoons dried white bread crumbs
1½ cups finely grated Gruyère or Swiss cheese

2 teaspoons Dijon mustard
½ teaspoon salt
½ teaspoon freshly ground black pepper
3 tablespoons all-purpose flour
1 cup plus 2 tablespoons milk
4 eggs, at room temperature, separated

Lightly grease the bottom and side of a 5½-cup soufflé dish that will fit in your freezer with butter until it is well coated.

Put the dish in the freezer 5 minutes to set the butter, then brush again with another small amount of butter and sprinkle with the bread crumbs. Rotate until the dish is well coated, then turn upside down and tap to remove any excess bread crumbs. Sprinkling the dish with bread crumbs helps the soufflé "grip" the side of the dish and rise evenly, and it also forms a delicate crust.

Heat the oven to 350°F. Put a cookie sheet on the lowest shelf in the oven, removing all the other shelves. (Heating the cookie sheet provides instant heat on the bottom of the soufflé and will help it to rise quickly and evenly.)

Put the cheese, mustard, salt and pepper in a heatproof bowl and leave to one side.

Melt the remaining butter in a saucepan over a medium heat until foaming. Add the flour and stir with a whisk 1 minute. [continued overleaf]

Whisk the butter and flour mixture until it forms a roux and starts to leave the side of the pan, but does not color. Remove the pan from the heat and add half the milk, whisking continuously until smooth. Gradually add the remaining milk, stirring until smooth. Cook over medium heat, stirring continuously, until the sauce is thick and boils. Reduce the heat to low and simmer the sauce, uncovered, 3 minutes, stirring occasionally, until thicker.

Pour the sauce over the cheese mixture and mix together. Add the egg yolks and mix until thoroughly combined.

Whisk the egg whites in a clean bowl until soft peaks form, taking care not to overwhisk or they will become dry and stiff, which makes them difficult to fold in and gives the soufflé a grainy texture.

Using a large metal spoon, fold one-quarter of the egg whites into the cheese sauce until just combined. Pour this mixture into one side of the bowl containing the egg whites (to minimize air loss), then fold in until just combined. The mixture should be spongy with streaks of egg white throughout, but without any large clumps of egg white.

Pour the mixture into the prepared soufflé dish and gently level the surface with a spatula. Run the back of a teaspoon around the inside rim of the dish and just into the soufflé mixture, creating a shallow furrow, which will help the soufflé rise evenly.

Put the soufflé dish on the hot cookie sheet and bake 45 minutes, or until the soufflé is well risen and slightly wobbly, and a skewer pushed through the side comes out clean and slightly moist. Serve immediately.

CHERRY CLAFOUTIS

All traditional clafoutis recipes use cherries with their pit still in, which lend a subtle hint of almond flavor to the dish, but you can remove them if you like. My mother was a real wizard at making clafoutis, whether with cherries, plums or small apricots, and this is her much-loved recipe.

Serves 4 to 6
Preparation time: 20 minutes
Cooking time: 40 to 50 minutes

butter, for greasing
scant 1 cup all-purpose flour, sifted,
  plus extra for dusting
12 ounces ripe sweet cherries, pitted
  if you like
2 tablespoons slivered almonds

3 eggs
½ cup plus 2 tablespoons sugar
1 tablespoon soft brown sugar
⅛ teaspoon salt
1 cup plus 2 tablespoons milk
2 teaspoons Amaretto or ¾ teaspoon
  almond extract
1½ teaspoons vanilla extract
confectioners' sugar, for dusting

Heat the oven to 350°F. Grease a 9- x 9-inch baking dish with butter, then lightly dust with some of the flour. Distribute the cherries and almonds in the prepared dish.

Whisk together the eggs, sugar, brown sugar, salt and the rest of the flour in a mixing bowl until smooth. Add the milk, Amaretto and vanilla extract, then whisk until smooth. Pour the batter over the cherries and almonds.

Bake 40 to 50 minutes until puffed up, light brown and a skewer inserted into the middle comes out clean. The clafoutis should tremble and shake a little when removed from the oven. Leave to cool slightly. Serve the clafoutis warm, dusted with confectioners' sugar.

The Sforza residence on Via Linneo.

8. THE TALE OF MOTHER SUPERIOR AND NANNY *Mischa*

Back in Rome, the family lived on Via Linneo, not far from the zoo and the Borghese Gardens. It was a newly built, charming house with a lovely garden. My mother, now aged nine, attended the nearby convent school, but soon even her day-to-day education seemed to get drawn into the political scene. But for both Fiammetta and Sforzino, the solid and unchanging presence of Nanny Mischa, waiting for them at home, was a huge comfort.

The situation at school was especially hard for Fiammetta because she was unpopular with the nuns, who supported Mussolini and knew all about Carlo's feelings concerning the dictator. My mother was forever being punished for the tiniest of misdemeanors with painful, humiliating rituals, such as kneeling for several hours in front of the statue of St. Anthony on a bed of rock salt. She was never able to bear the thought of that particular saint after that, and she never forgot the pain from her cut knees as the salt seeped into her wounds.

My favorite story from my mother's school days involved the mother superior and a large tureen of bean soup. One day, my mother was given the job of dishing out the soup to the rest of her table. She lifted the lid from the tureen and dipped in the ladle. As she did so, she glanced down at the soup. To her disgust, the beans were moving—they had small maggots wriggling out of them. Fiammetta put down the ladle, replaced the lid on the tureen and waited for mother superior to come to the table. In a moment she was by her side, demanding to know why my mother was not carrying out her duty. Fiammetta explained that she had seen maggots in the soup, but the mother superior refused to believe her, accused her of lying and ordered her to serve the soup.

> **The situation at school was especially hard for Fiammetta because she was unpopular with the nuns, who supported Mussolini.**

With that, Fiammetta lifted up the heavy tureen and tipped the soup over the nun's head, making sure she was well-covered in the maggoty beans.

This incident resulted in several more agonizing hours spent on her knees in front of St. Anthony before going home to the gentle ministrations of Mischa and her mother, and a supper of her favorite *Bucatini all'Amatriciana* (Spicy Tomato & Pancetta Pasta, see page 95) and a simple but comforting *Crostata di Marmellata* (Jam Tart, see page 99), made with her favorite homemade Fig Jam (see page 99).

The Sforza children were repeatedly harassed on their way to school. As Carlo's children, they were also under suspicion and Blackshirt soldiers rifled through their satchels almost on a daily basis. Sforzino would sometimes fight back by playing tricks on the soldiers, planting frogs in his satchel that would obligingly jump out and startle the guards.

At home, things were getting more difficult by the day. The family's mail was censored and their phone was tapped. Whenever Valentine received a call in a foreign language, the operator would come on the line and tell her to stop speaking until they found the right interpreter to listen in; sometimes my grandmother would pick up the telephone to be greeted by a string of dreadful obscenities. Her faithful Hungarian housemaid, Fanny, was instructed to hand over the contents of the wastepaper baskets each day to the authorities for examination. She also had to keep careful notes on all household conversations, especially those around the dining table, and report back daily to the guards on duty at their gates. Every time Carlo went for a walk, there would be a guard walking behind him. Occasionally, my grandfather would tease him: in hot weather, he would airily hand the guard his coat, remarking: "At least you can make yourself useful."

In the midst of all this, the Sforza parents appeared calm and in control. Nothing seemed to shake their resolve to fight the oppression with dignity. In the evenings, the family would gather for supper—simple meals of soup, followed by broiled fish or meat. None of them had much appetite for anything elaborate or festive during those dark days. If Carlo and Valentine were out for dinner, the children would eat their supper in the nursery with Mischa. My mother hated spinach, which her brother loved, and if it was served they would deftly swop plates when Mischa's back was turned.

Carlo and Valentine wrapped the family in a cocoon of love. Even when things were at their most difficult for him, Carlo still found time to have a mimosa tree planted below Valentine's bedroom balcony, like the one she had so loved in Peking. My grandmother also managed to rise above the

Top: Nonno Carlo and Nanny Mischa
with Fiammetta on the beach.
Above, Sforzino and Fiammetta in the garden.

tension and maintain a serene home: one afternoon my mother remembered returning to find the delicious scent of freesias together with the sound of her mother's piano-playing wafting through the house. Carlo had asked the gardener to plant a whole bed of the flowers under the sitting room windows, just because Valentine loved them.

At some point, however, it became impossible to maintain a calm and happy home. One night, after another of Carlo's inflammatory speeches in the Senate, there was an especially rowdy and vicious attack on the family. A gang of young Fascists, armed with buckets of muck, forced their way into the

A gang of young Fascists, armed with buckets of muck, forced their way into the house.

house. They began to throw great handfuls of it at the painting of Carlo, in full diplomatic uniform, which hung in the hallway. Valentine, her long hair hanging down her back, dressed only in her nightdress, stood on the stairs and shouted at them, "What kind of men are you? I am alone in the house with my children!"

Fiammetta tried to remain strong, but a few days later, unable to bear school a moment longer, she ran away. She had been asked to carry the Fascist flag in the Madonna procession and, when it was handed to her, she had stamped and spat on it. Hours of brutal punishment followed and when she was finally released, she took off. A few days later, her knees still sore from her punishment, a ball was thrown over the school wall accidentally during a tennis game. Fiammetta climbed over to fetch it and headed straight home, never to return.

I have added my family's time-honored and dearly loved recipe for *Pasta e Fagioli* (Bean & Pasta Soup, see page 96) because, despite the dreadful experience that my mother suffered with that tureen of soup at the hands of the mother superior when she was at school, this dish has always been a mainstay of my family's meals, served hot in winter and lightly chilled in summer. It is far too comforting, delicious and important to leave out. My mother, in recounting the story of the school soup, always remarked that nuns in Italy have a reputation for enjoying their food and doubtless would have eaten something much more palatable in their own private dining room.

SPICY TOMATO & PANCETTA PASTA

This dish comes from the small town of Amatrice, in Lazio, and was a favorite Sforza family meal when they lived in Rome. Bucatini are fat, hollow spaghetti, perfect for absorbing robust sauces, but you can also use ordinary spaghetti if you prefer. In most tomato-based sauces, Italians like to use either garlic or onion; it is rare to find both in the same dish. I have taken part in many discussions about which is the best type of bacon to use in this dish—many favor pancetta, which is made from the belly, while others prefer the cured and salted guanciale, the cheek of the pig. While you can use Parmesan, the cheese of choice would be the saltier and more peppery Pecorino Romano.

Serves 4
Preparation time: 15 minutes
Cooking time: 40 minutes

3 tablespoons extra virgin olive oil
10 ounces thickly cut pancetta or
  guanciale, cubed
1 onion, finely chopped
3 garlic cloves, chopped
½ to 2 dry red chilies, according to
  taste, seeded and finely chopped

5 tablespoons dry white wine
1 can (15-oz.) plum tomatoes,
  chopped
14 ounces dry bucatini
kosher salt
¾ cup freshly grated Pecorino
  Romano, to serve

Heat the oil in a large skillet over medium-high heat. Add the pancetta and fry until the fat is transparent and running freely. Add the onion, garlic and chili, then reduce the heat and fry gently 10 minutes, stirring occasionally, or until the onion is soft and translucent.

Add the wine and leave to bubble a few minutes. Add the tomatoes and simmer, covered, 30 minutes, stirring frequently, or until the sauce is thick and glossy. Season lightly with salt.

Meanwhile, bring a large saucepan of salted water to a boil. Add the pasta and cook according to the package directions until al dente. Drain and return the pasta to the pan, then pour in the sauce and mix together well. Serve with grated Pecorino for adding at the table.

BEAN & PASTA SOUP

This has become one of my family's most dearly loved recipes, despite my mother's dreadful experience at school! If you use fresh beans in their pods, they will need to be shelled, soaked and treated like dry beans, although cooked for a little less time, or you can use canned beans. Beppino always added a special wild herb he picked for the soup, called *puerin* in the local dialect, but I think it was probably *nepitella*, known as "lesser calamint" in English.

Serves 4
Preparation time: about 15 minutes, plus at least 8 hours soaking
Cooking time: 2 to 2½ hours

1½ cups dry beans, preferably borlotti, soaked in cold water at least 8 hours
2 tablespoons olive oil
2½ ounces thickly sliced pancetta or prosciutto, cubed
1 onion, chopped
1 carrot, chopped
1 celery stick, chopped
6 cups strong meat stock
⅔ cup dry soup pasta
kosher salt and freshly ground black pepper
good-quality extra virgin olive oil and freshly grated Parmesan cheese, to serve

Bring a covered saucepan of unsalted water to a boil. Drain and rinse the beans, add them to the pan and boil hard 10 minutes, then drain and rinse again. Return the beans to the pan, cover with fresh unsalted water and bring to a boil. Reduce the heat and simmer gently 45 to 60 minutes until tender, then drain.

Heat the oil in a large saucepan over medium heat. Add the pancetta, onion, carrot and celery and fry 5 to 10 minutes until the vegetables are soft. Add the beans and stir well.

Pour in the stock and bring to a boil, then reduce the heat and simmer 45 to 50 minutes until the beans are almost falling apart. Add the pasta and cook 10 minutes longer, or until tender.

Season with salt and pepper and serve warm with a drizzle of extra virgin olive oil and grated Parmesan for adding at the table.

JAM TART

Serves 8
Preparation time: 30 minutes,
  plus making the jam and
  30 minutes chilling
Cooking time: 40 minutes

Piecrust:
1 egg, plus 2 egg yolks, beaten
½ cup plus 2 tablespoons sugar, plus
  extra for sprinkling
2 cups all-purpose flour, sifted, plus
  extra as needed and for dusting
1 stick (½ cup) unsalted butter,
  melted, plus extra for greasing

finely grated zest of 1 unwaxed lemon
½ teaspoon baking powder
1 teaspoon vanilla extract
2 tablespoons milk, for brushing

Fig jam (fills two 1-pound jars):
2 pounds black or green figs, rinsed
  and quartered
1¾ cups preserving or granulated
  sugar
juice and finely grated zest of
  2 unwaxed lemons

To make the jam, put all the ingredients in a stainless-steel preserving pan or large, heavy-based saucepan and simmer gently 1 to 1½ hours, stirring occasionally. To test if the jam is set, drop a teaspoonful of the mixture onto a cold saucer and cool slightly, then push with your fingertip—the surface should wrinkle and the mixture remain firm. Remove the pan from the heat and transfer the jam to hot, dry sterilized jars (see *Cook's Note*, page 40). Seal immediately and leave to cool. Store in a cool, dark place until required.

To make the piecrust dough, beat together the egg, egg yolks and sugar in a mixing bowl until light and fluffy, then gradually mix in the remaining pastry ingredients, except the milk. Using wet hands, quickly combine to form a soft dough, sprinkling with a little more flour if the dough is too sticky. Wrap the dough in plastic wrap and chill 30 minutes.

Heat the oven to 350°F. Grease a shallow 9-inch tart pan with a removeable base with butter, then lightly dust with flour. Roll out three-quarters of the dough into a circle a little larger than the tart pan, then use it to line the pan. Press it evenly into the pan, making sure it comes up to the top. Roll out the remaining dough, then cut into thin strips to make a lattice.

Spoon enough of the fig jam into the tart case to fill it almost to the top, then spread it out with the back of a spoon. Lay the dough strips on top to create a lattice, then brush the dough with a little milk. Bake in the middle of the oven 40 minutes, or until the pastry is golden brown. Leave to cool slightly in the pan, then remove and sprinkle with a little sugar. Serve warm or cold.

Top: Le Grand Pin, the family retreat
in the South of France.
Above, Fiammetta in contemplative mood.

9.   ESCAPE TO BELGIUM AND THE COMFORTS OF LE *Grand Pin*

On June 10, 1924, Giacomo Matteotti, one of the bravest Italians who ever dared to speak out against Mussolini, simply disappeared. Two months later his body was found just outside Rome. A carpenter's file had been driven into his chest. Matteotti had been the head of the Italian Socialist Party and, like my Nonno, had not been afraid to speak his mind. For this, he had paid with his life.

Real, cold terror now gripped the Sforza family, who were still living on Via Linneo. My Nonno, now aged fifty-six, was repeatedly attacked, before being dumped on the doorstep of his home, bloodied and bruised. Over and over again, the Blackshirts forced their way into the house, smashing the Sforzas' precious possessions indiscriminately. Then, in October 1926, their much-loved family home on the Tuscan coast was torched and burned to the ground.

It was clear that the family had to leave Italy for their own safety. Carlo was determined to continue the fight against Fascism from abroad by writing and lecturing. In March 1927, after much careful planning—and after many influential friends had been contacted and persuaded to help—Carlo set sail for Peking on the pretext of having been commissioned by the *Manchester Guardian* and the *Journal des Débats* to write various articles. Few people knew he was actually leaving for good, and the Fascist authorities, although suspicious, were eventually persuaded he would return. Carlo left his wife and children behind, with Nanny Mischa and the rest of the servants, under terrifying conditions of increasing harassment and oppression.

> It was clear the family had to leave Italy for their own safety. Carlo was determined to continue the fight against Fascism from abroad...

Once Valentine knew that Carlo was safe, she made plans for her own escape. She enlisted the assistance of her sister Germaine, who was living in Brussels with their father. Knowing her sister's mail was opened and read by the Blackshirts, Germaine helped to prepare the ground for the family's escape, sending a stream of increasingly anguished letters to Valentine, begging her to come to Brussels at once to see their dying father. In fact, although their father was very ill, his condition was not life-threatening, but the ruse worked: Valentine was able to escape.

Once the Fascist authorities had checked Count Gaston Charles Errembault de Dudzeele was indeed Valentine's father, and that he appeared to be on his deathbed, Valentine was allowed to leave, but on the condition that she left her children behind. This was torment for her. Torn between the knowledge that this was the only way to get out—and get her children out after her—and the terrible wrench of leaving her children behind, she was paralyzed. Eventually, it was Mischa who persuaded her to go—although she too was aware of the danger she and the children were facing. She was adamant that she would get them to Belgium safely.

Before leaving Italy, Valentine made arrangements with various well-connected friends who could help Nanny Mischa and the children to leave safely. She reassured Fiammetta and Sforzino, promising they would all be together in Belgium soon, and urged them to be courageous and strong. As Valentine boarded a train at Rome's Stazione Termini, the children, comforted by Nanny Mischa, promised they would be brave for the sake of their mother.

Valentine's train journey across France went smoothly enough, and soon she was back in her own country, reunited with her sister Germaine and her father in Brussels. The following month the little party of three—my mother, uncle and Nanny Mischa—set off on the first leg of their journey from Rome. At first they did not encounter any problems, but they soon ran into difficulties on the French border at Modane. The children and their nanny were dragged roughly off the train and were ordered to stand on the platform in the dark, while the Fascist border officials interrogated them. Nanny Mischa took control of the situation. While the children shrank back against the skirts of her uniform, scared but nonetheless determined to keep their promise to their mother to be brave, the Blackshirts circled the little group, stamping their boots, their taunts and insults growing more ominous by the minute. Mischa drew herself up to her full height. "Leave us alone!" she said. "These children are in my care!"

Her tone had the desired effect. The guards drew aside to confer, then—although they held on to Mischa for questioning—they let the children board

Some of my Belgian cousins!

the train. It had been imperative that they caught it: on it, unbeknown to the Blackshirts, were a handful of people waiting to help the children. Once on board, they were quickly hidden from view as the train began to pull out of the station. My mother remembered spending the rest of the journey rolled up in a stranger's coat, lying on a hard coat-rack and barely daring to breathe. All across France, an unmarked car followed the train, its headlights visible from the carriage windows.

> The threat of German invasion hung over the party, even while they enjoyed long, lazy Provençal lunches...

At last, the long and terrible journey was over. As the train pulled into Brussels Central, the sight of their mother standing on the platform was almost too much for the exhausted children to bear. Overwhelmed with relief, Valentine held them tight. They were safe, and their seventeen-year exile had begun.

Nanny Mischa joined them shortly after, having withstood her interrogation stoically, and the family settled into Valentine's father's house at 4, Rue de la Grosse Tour. It was a few months before Carlo could join them: he needed to keep well away from the tentacles of Mussolini's regime, so stayed a few months longer in China, waiting for the dust to settle. When the family were together once more, they divided their time between Brussels and their home in the South of France called Le Grand Pin. This would be the case for the next ten years, until World War II made it impossible.

Carlo, unemployed apart from writing his many books and journals about European politics, needed to earn a living, so spent each academic year away from Valentine and the children on various lecture tours, including several to the United States. Each summer, when he was back for the holiday months, Le Grand Pin became a place where freethinking intellectuals gathered to enjoy long discussions over lunch on the terrace and swims in the little private cove at the foot of the cliffs. My mother remembered meeting Thomas Mann, among the crowd of bohemian artists, writers in crisis and various hangers-on that filled the house to overflowing.

Through these sundrenched summer months, Fiammetta always sensed an undercurrent of fear. The threat of German invasion hung over the party, even while they enjoyed long, lazy Provençal lunches, the table covered in brightly painted bowls of ratatouille, stuffed zucchini, *la Bouillabaisse* with its little bowls of *rouille* (see page 107), and dense, green *tourte de blettes* (Swiss chard, raisin and pine nut tart).

Life in Brussels was more sedate. For my mother, it was punctuated by school, homework and the simple comforts and daily customs of family life. Mischa was a constant, unwavering presence, imposing routine, regular meals, spotlessly clean hands and good manners. They all tried very hard to live as normal a life as possible, even in the shadow of the increasingly militant Fascists, and this was helped by the steady ritual of regular meals at the carefully laid table, adding a reliable rhythm to each day.

My mother would often tell me about the food she discovered and came to enjoy during those years in Belgium, especially the huge mounds of tiny boiled brown shrimp she would watch the market traders shell, their hands flying so fast in the cold air they were almost a blur, before wrapping them expertly in brown paper. Many years later, when my mother lived with us in Norfolk, in England, and my boys were just babies, I would buy shrimp, knowing how much she loved them. Inevitably, though, my gesture would provoke such an outpouring of memories for her that it almost made me regret my purchase. From my mother, I learned early and hard about the link that exists between food and buried memories: she showed me how the taste of a particular food can transport you, instantly, to another place and time.

Knowing all I know now, I think this period in Belgium, punctuated by the family's holidays in Provence, gave them all some much-needed space to recover from the horrors they had left behind when they closed the front door of their home on Via Linneo for the last time. Mischa remained with the children, even after they were too old for a nanny, continuing to offer much-needed stability, and Valentine took much solace in the companionship of her sister.

> **They all tried very hard to live as normal a life as possible, even in the shadow of the increasingly militant Fascists...**

Carlo traveled extensively. There is a photograph somewhere of him sitting on a beach in Argentina with Eva Perón, and there was always gossip of him being seen with other women. The rumors of his many alleged indiscretions filtered through to Valentine, but she never stopped loving and supporting him. As she said to my mother: *"On n'aime pas si l'on n'aime pour toujours."* (You must never love him, if not forever.)

Many years later, when I was a little girl eager to absorb my mother's foodie enthusiasm, we would spend rainy winter afternoons in her kitchen making mountains of golden galettes, using my Nonna's heavy waffle iron over the gas stove. My mother would drizzle the thin batter over the hot metal before clamping the iron shut, counting to sixty, then heaving it over onto the other side with two hands to repeat the whole process. Another minute, and the iron would be opened to reveal a wafer-thin galette. The three of us—my mother, my Nonna and I—would then dip them into bowls of hot chocolate.

My Nonna, with her love of all things sweet and sticky, also enjoyed *Pâté de Coing* (Quince Cheese, see page 111), a passion that lasted well into her later years. I remember her offering me those dark amber-colored cubes, lightly dusted in confectioners' sugar, as a special fall treat, when quinces were in season. I have inherited her love of quinces and can never prepare them without thinking of her. I especially like to bake them slowly with sugar and water until they are spoonably soft and almost garnet-red.

Nonno Carlo and Great Aunt Lili.

LA BOUILLABAISSE

Bouillabaisse is one of the great dishes of French Provençal cuisine and one that my grandparents often served to guests at their home, Le Grand Pin, in the south of France. When I recently talked about this recipe with my family and the memories it inevitably brings out in us, there was much discussion around our table as to whether or not a traditional *bouillabaisse* should be served with *rouille*, or whether this garlicky sauce is only ever served with *soupe au poissons*. As far as I know, *rouille* can be served with both, so I have included it here because I know how much my mother would love to spread it onto thin slices of crisp baguette. According to my mother, *bouillabaisse* should ideally also include rascasse, an ugly, bony rock fish found only in the Mediterranean, but feel free to make it with any combination of fish and seafood available to you—the selection needs to be as varied as possible.

Serves 6
Preparation time: 45 minutes
Cooking time: 1 hour 15 minutes

6 pounds mixed fish and shellfish,
   such as halibut, mullet, shrimp,
   mussels and clams, cleaned,
   prepared and filleted
1 large French baguette, sliced
1 tablespoon roughly chopped parsley

Fish broth:
4 tablespoons olive oil
1 large onion, chopped
2 celery sticks, chopped
4 garlic cloves, crushed
about 2½ pounds fish heads
   and bones
3½ cups chopped ripe tomatoes
1 fennel bulb, trimmed and chopped,
   or 1 teaspoon dried fennel seeds

3¼-inch strip of orange peel, white
   pith removed
8 parsley sprigs
2 thyme sprigs
1 bay leaf
a pinch of saffron threads
2 teaspoons kosher salt
6 to 8 black peppercorns
1¾ cups white wine

Rouille:
1 potato, unpeeled and left whole
1 red bell pepper
4 garlic cloves, crushed
1 red chili, seeded and finely chopped
⅓ cup olive oil
kosher salt and freshly ground
   black pepper

First, make the broth. Heat the oil in a large saucepan over medium heat. Add the onion, celery and garlic and fry gently until the onions are soft and translucent. [continued overleaf]

Stir in the remaining broth ingredients, then bring to a boil and boil briefly to cook off the alcohol in the wine. Pour in 1⅔ cups water or enough to cover all the broth ingredients in the pan. Return to a boil, then reduce the heat to low and simmer 30 to 40 minutes. Strain through a strainer into a heatproof pitcher, discarding the solids, and add a little more salt and pepper, if you like. If not using immediately, leave to cool and chill, covered, up to 2 days.

To make the rouille, heat the broiler to high. Put the potato in a saucepan, cover with water and bring to a boil. Boil 15 minutes, or until it is tender, then drain. Meanwhile, broil the red pepper 10 minutes, turning frequently, until charred all over. Put in a plastic food bag, seal and leave 5 minutes. When cool, peel away the blackened skin.

Cut the broiled pepper in half and remove the seeds. Put the pepper, potato, garlic and chili in a blender or food processor with a little of the broth and season with salt and pepper. With the machine running, gradually pour in the oil, adding a little more of the broth if needed, until the mixture is thick but spreadable. Add a little more salt and pepper, if you like, then transfer to a small bowl and leave to one side.

Scrub the mussels and clams thoroughly with a stiff brush under cold running water to remove all traces of grit, then remove any barnacles or other debris attached to the shells and pull off and discard the "beard" from the mussels. Rinse the shellfish again and discard any with broken shells or that do not close as soon as they are tapped.

Put the broth in a saucepan and bring to a simmer over medium heat. Add the fish and shellfish in batches, starting with the firmest fish first, such as halibut and mullet, and ending with the most delicate shellfish, such as the shrimp, mussels and clams. Simmer until all the seafood is cooked and any shells have opened, about 8 to 10 minutes. Discard any shells that remain closed.

Meanwhile, heat the broiler to medium. Broil the slices of baguette until golden and toasted. To serve, put 2 or 3 slices of toasted baguette in the bottom of each of six bowls. Spoon the fish and seafood into the bowls, then ladle the broth over. Sprinkle with parsley and serve with the rouille for adding at the table.

BROWN SHRIMP OMELET

This was one of my mother's favorite dishes, and I can see why—the eggs and little brown shrimp come together so perfectly in this lovely recipe of hers, which is reminiscent of her time in Belgium. You can, of course, make four separate two-egg omelets instead of one large eight-egg omelet as below.

Serves 4
Preparation time: 5 minutes
Cooking time: 10 minutes

8 extra-large eggs
a splash of milk
3 tablespoons unsalted butter

5 ounces cooked and shelled brown
   shrimp
2 tablespoons snipped chives
kosher salt and freshly ground
   black pepper
Belgian endive salad, to serve

Beat the eggs in a large bowl until only just combined, then stir in a pinch of salt, pepper and a splash of milk.

Melt the butter in a large, nonstick omelet pan or skillet over medium heat. As soon as the butter melts and stops sizzling, but is not brown, pour in the egg mixture and tilt the pan so it covers the base. Cook the omelet until the egg is mostly set on the bottom but is still runny on top, especially in the middle.

Scatter the shrimp and chives over the top, then flip the omelet in half to encase them. Cook 2 minutes longer to just heat through, moving the pan around to prevent anything from catching or burning. Serve the omelet with a Belgian endive salad.

QUINCE CHEESE

Pâté de coing (*la cotognata* in Italian) is a lovely, old-fashioned French delicacy made by boiling quinces, the very last of fall fruits, and then leaving them to set into a sticky, sweet, thick jelly. In France (and Italy), it is one of the great traditional sweetmeats of the fall. My Nonna always loved it: she also used ripe quinces to scent her linen cupboard and often had a bowl of the fragrant fruit sitting on a table to fill the house with their delicate perfume.

Makes about 1 pound
Preparation time: 30 minutes
Cooking time: 45 minutes

1 pound 2 ounces quinces, peeled,
  cored and sliced
1¾ cups superfine sugar
juice of 1 lemon
confectioners' sugar or superfine
  sugar, for dusting

Put the quinces, sugar and lemon juice in a stainless-steel preserving pan or large, heavy-based saucepan with 3 tablespoons water and bring to a gentle simmer, then simmer 40 minutes, stirring occasionally, or until the fruit break down into a thick, smooth puree. If necessary, blitz the mixture briefly with a hand-held blender to remove any lumps.

To test the mixture, drop a teaspoonful onto a cold saucer and then tilt the saucer. If the mixture remains solid, the quince cheese is ready. If not, continue to simmer the mixture an extra 5 minutes and test again.

Pour the mixture into a shallow baking tray lined with parchment paper and leave to cool and set. Once solid and cold, cut into small squares and dust with confectioners' sugar to serve. If not serving immediately, layer the quince cheese in an airtight container, interleaved with wax paper, and store in a cool place up to 1 week.

CLASSIC BELGIAN COOKIES

My mother loved baking cookies, and my brothers and I grew up loving these very special, lightly spiced treats, so lovingly made for us to enjoy with a cup of tea or to dunk shamelessly into bowls of decadently rich, hot chocolate. Although traditionally these cookies are sandwiched together with jam and then lightly frosted, I must say I have always preferred eating them plain.

Makes about 24 plain or
  10 filled cookies
Preparation time: 15 to 25 minutes,
  plus 30 minutes chilling and
  10 minutes cooling
Cooking time: 10 to 15 minutes

1¾ cups packed soft light brown
  sugar
2¼ sticks (1 cup plus 2 tablespoons)
  unsalted butter, softened
1 egg
2½ teaspoons apple pie spice

1½ teaspoons ground cinnamon
3 cups all-purpose flour, sifted
1 teaspoon baking powder
4 tablespoons strawberry jam
  (optional)
hot chocolate, to serve (optional)

Frosting (optional):
1½ cups confectioners' sugar
1 tablespoon milk
1 teaspoon unsalted butter, melted

Put the brown sugar, butter and egg in a food processor and process until well combined. Add the apple pie spice, cinnamon, flour and baking powder and pulse until the mixture combines to form a dough. Divide the dough in half, then shape into two 4-inch-thick logs. Wrap each log separately in plastic wrap and chill 30 minutes, or until firm.

Heat the oven to 350°F and line 2 large cookie sheets with wax paper. Roll out each piece of dough between 2 sheets of wax paper until ¼ inch thick, then stamp out circles using a 2½-inch cookie cutter if making plain cookies, or a 1½-inch cookie cutter if making filled cookies, rerolling the trimmings as necessary.

Put the cookies on the prepared cookie sheets and bake 10 to 15 minute until golden. Leave to cool on the sheets 5 minutes, then transfer to a wire rack to cool completely.

Meanwhile, make the frosting, if using. Sift the confectioners' sugar into a small bowl, then add the milk and butter. Beat vigorously until the mixture is well combined and spreadable. If it is too stiff, add a little more milk. Spread half the cooled cookies with the jam, if using, then sandwich together with the remaining cookies. Spread the frosting over the top and leave to set slightly for a few minutes. Alternatively, serve the cookies plain with a cup of rich, hot chocolate.

The swimming pool at the house in Cape Cod,
where the Sforzas stayed during the war.

10.   EXILE ON CAPE COD AND TEA WITH *Eleanor*

The Sforzas' relatively peaceful period of exile in Brussels and the South of France came to an abrupt end with the start of World War II. With Mussolini firmly allied to Hitler, and both Belgium and France on the brink of invasion, the family had to escape once again. The stability of their life in Brussels and the idyll of summers in the South of France, with those long, relaxed Provençal lunches, were unfortunately over.

The family drove as far as Normandy, where they joined forces with a group of Italian friends and some of Carlo's political allies. Here, they lived for six or seven months in simple, rented accommodation, waiting anxiously and listening to the radio for daily developments. By September 1940, it became all too obvious the Germans were advancing fast, so the family hastened southwest by road to Bordeaux in a convoy of cars, frequently buzzed by enemy planes. In Bordeaux, they went immediately to the British consulate. Fortunately, the British consul was a long-time admirer of Carlo's, so they were warmly welcomed, given dinner—with plenty of red wine to fortify them—and promised a safe passage to England as soon as possible.

The only available boat was a Dutch cargo ship returning from South America, loaded with linseed. She had already attempted to dock at both Amsterdam and Rotterdam, only to find the Germans had destroyed both ports. The ship was now bound for Falmouth, and the captain told Carlo he could take 60 passengers, including the Sforzas, but warned him there would not be any food on board. As he also told them the crossing was going to take about four days, finding something to eat was vital. Fiammetta and her brother were sent out into the chaos of the panic-stricken city to buy whatever they could find with the few francs the family had left. They returned with ten oranges, six bananas, four cans of sardines and three baguettes. My mother was never able to eat a banana again for the rest of her life.

> **With Mussolini firmly allied to Hitler, and both Belgium and France on the brink of invasion, the family had to escape once again.**

The British sailors working in the port, anxious to destroy any evidence of their whereabouts and make sure the family's trail was well and truly cold, pushed the cars—loaded with the possessions they could not take on board —deep into the water. The family, standing on the quayside with just a few essential items, told each other they would rather lose everything than leave their precious possessions behind to be crudely picked over by the enemy.

The ship set sail, with its extra cargo of people, and traveled up through the estuary and across the English Channel, the captain dodging the enemy deftly. Most of her passengers were in the hold, hidden among the linseed sacks. The Sforzas' traveling companions were a strange bunch: butlers, valets, nannies, priests and—by some odd chance—several Royal Lancers. Like the Sforzas, they had hung on until the very last minute before evacuating.

Valentine was given a basic cabin on board, but Carlo and the children made the best of it in the hold among the linseed sacks. My mother remembers being too worried and afraid to relax, and the mixture of engine fumes and linseed did nothing to help her lifelong propensity for seasickness. Four days later they docked in Cornwall, where the Women's Voluntary Service met them in Falmouth harbor, giving each passenger a slip of paper, on which was an address of someone who would give them a hot meal and a bed for the night, without asking questions. Exhausted and shaken, every trace of her usual sparkle gone, twenty-five-year-old Fiammetta appeared on the doorstep of a complete stranger and was given the most caring, unconditional welcome she had experienced in her life. She slept solidly for thirty-eight hours in a spotlessly clean room, only woken by her hostess when it was time to board the blacked-out train to London. After a substantial breakfast of kippers, eggs and several cups of very strong tea, Fiammetta was driven to the railroad station where she joined her family on the train headed for London.

Once in London, the family was hidden in the back bedroom of a house for a few days. After dark, mysterious strangers would visit, whose job it was to secure their safe passage to the United States. The only contact they had with their host was the mysterious appearance of trays, bearing tea and a couple of thin, fish-paste sandwiches, which were left outside the door.

Very early, on an icy winter's morning, the family set off by road for Liverpool, where they boarded the *Duchess of Atoll*, bound for Quebec. Their voyage across the Atlantic was slow and filled with almost unbearable anxiety due to the U-boats and planes patroling the waters. They were thankful for

Fiammetta, far left in New York with friends from the Red Cross.

the forced inactivity it offered, though, as the crossing allowed them to take advantage of some rest and regular small meals of simple food. When they docked in Canada, an official car met them. They loaded their few remaining possessions into it and headed for the border, ready to begin their new life in the United States of America.

At the border, the family was suddenly and unexpectedly separated once again. This time it was Fiammetta's Chinese birth certificate that was the problem. She was detained in Quebec while the authorities researched her background and, after a few days of waiting, she was informed that the American consul was ill in bed with measles. The vice consul, determined to perform his duties meticulously, was adamant Fiammetta would remain in Canada "until the matter has been researched scrupulously and checked down to the very last detail." No amount of pleading or reasoning would change his mind.

> **Their voyage across the Atlantic was slow and filled with almost unbearable anxiety due to the U-boats...**

As soon as Carlo reached Washington, he contacted the White House. One phone call later, and miraculously the vice consul at the Canadian border disappeared and the consul, mercifully free of measles, reappeared. He took Fiammetta and another girl, who had also been detained, out for a luxurious dinner of lobster tails and a slice of *tarte au sucre*, the famous sugar and maple syrup pie of Quebec. When they boarded the train for Washington, the two girls were given vast bouquets of flowers and a thousand apologies.

President Roosevelt, who had long since admired Carlo's political views and had read many of his books, instructed his officials to make sure the Sforzas reached their new home on Cape Cod safely. The family loved their comfortable house and the quaint seaside town with its clapboard houses and white-steepled church. Surrounded by the serenity of this peaceful place, with its long sandy beaches, they felt far away from the troubles in Europe and thankful for the extraordinary generosity of the Americans. The Sforzas felt safer than they had in a long time. Cape Cod was a haven, with a glorious abundance of seafood and delicious, creamy, comforting chowders that assuaged their longing for the familiar things of home.

Carlo, feeling unable to accept this gift from the American government without giving something in return, spent a great deal of his time either writing, or touring various universities as a guest lecturer, most often to Columbia. Valentine, exhausted by all the near-misses and the long, cold fear she had suffered over the past few years, spent her time reading and resting when she was not traveling with her husband. She became a good friend of Eleanor Roosevelt, with whom she shared many of the same political views regarding women and their rights, and she often stayed in Washington, drinking tea and eating cakes with the First Lady and her entourage.

Fiammetta recovered very quickly from her ordeal and felt the need to explore the United States. She moved to New York City, taught herself to cook by listening to the "Mystery Chef" on the radio, trained as a Red Cross nurse and took a job at the Metropolitan Opera, teaching opera singers how to pronounce Italian correctly. She also volunteered to feed soldiers returning from the war, those who could not use their hands or were blinded. She told me this was a job that required a very strong stomach and endless patience, but that it kept her in touch with what was going on in Europe—the wounded told her their stories as she spooned soup into their mouths.

New York was the center of activity in the United States during World War II. When Hitler came to power in Germany, American Nazis were to be seen goose-stepping in Yorkville, on the Upper East Side, while recently arrived Jewish immigrants found much-needed refuge on the Upper West Side. Once America joined the fight, enlisted men heading for Europe or the Pacific streamed through Grand Central Terminal and Pennsylvania Station, and soldiers crowded into Times Square to enjoy their precious free time. The Brooklyn Navy Yard refitted many ships, some of which were attacked by German U-boats as the convoys left New York Harbor. Silhouetted against the skyline, they were easy pickings and, after weeks of fatalities—with debris and bodies being regularly washed up on Long Island's beaches—the city finally imposed a stringent dimming of the lights.

> **She became a good friend of Eleanor Roosevelt, with whom she shared many of the same political views...**

Despite the war, the stifling heat in summer, the freezing winters, the fact that Americans apparently ate persimmons with mayonnaise and the thousands of cockroaches in her apartment, Fiammetta genuinely loved New York City. She made many dear friends there, including Arthur Hays Sulzberger, publisher of *The New York Times*, and his wife Iphigene, who visited my parents in Rome several times over a period of many years. (Mrs. Sulzberger always stayed at the incredibly luxurious Hotel Hassler Villa Medici on Trinità dei Monti. I remember when I was a gauche, pimply teenager, having dinner in its dining room, as a guest of the wonderfully gracious Signora Sulzberger, feeling amazed by the heart-stopping views over the Spanish Steps and the rooftops of Rome. I watched shyly as the handsome waiters filleted our sea bass for us at the table, and flambéed a steak with theatrical panache.)

Some of the first recipes my mother taught me to make were from her battered collection of American cookbooks she brought home from the United States. It was a magical time, alone with her in the kitchen of our apartment in Rome, learning about creaming butter and sugar with the back of a wooden spoon, or how to measure butter by adding it to cold water in a measuring jug and watching the water level rise. My favorite of my mother's American books was *Learn to Bake! You'll Love it!* Even now I am comfortable using cup measurements, as a result of my being introduced to American cookbooks so early on.

Childhood Sunday afternoon cooking sessions with my mother involved much baking—especially pies, cookies and cakes—peppered by stories of her wartime experiences, especially how hard it had been to get the Italian ingredients she craved to make the kind of food she needed for comfort and reassurance. I understood exactly how she felt—when I first moved to London in the mid-1970s, it was much harder than it is today to find the Italian ingredients I wanted. A simple risotto, sprinkled with fresh Parmesan, was desperately longed for, and often enough to stop the pangs of homesickness that so often threatened to engulf me completely.

Although my mother could seldom afford to eat out in New York, when she lived there in the 1940s, there were always the Americanized versions of Italian dishes that were served in the many Italian restaurants, and she would often shop in Little Italy, hunting out ingredients such as olive oil, pasta wrapped in blue paper or canned Italian tomatoes, which were even more of a rarity during the war. Rather incongruously, she maintained a great fondness for ice-cream sodas and the delights of the soda fountain, and introduced me proudly, many years later, to the joys of a Brown Cow. I cannot say I shared my mother's enthusiasm, and found the combination of Coca-Cola and vanilla ice cream to be absolutely disgusting. But then, unlike her, I had never had one in New York in the 1940s.

All the time the Sforza family were in exile in the United States, they kept careful track of what was happening at home in Italy, through letters from their family and friends, as well as snippets of unofficial news through the White House and the press. Carlo always vowed he would return home the moment Italy surrendered to the Allied forces and, straight after the Armistice, he took one of the first postwar transatlantic passenger flights back. He took Sforzino with him, while Valentine and Fiammetta stayed behind, waiting until a safe passage could be arranged on a ship.

Fiammetta in New York.

CHICKEN POTPIE

Serves 6
Preparation time: 30 minutes, plus
    cooling and 15 minutes standing
Cooking time: 1 hour 10 minutes

2 tablespoons sunflower oil, plus
    extra for greasing
3 skinless, boneless chicken breast
    halves
2 carrots, sliced
4 celery sticks, sliced
3 potatoes, peeled and cut into
    ½-inch cubes
1 cup frozen peas
1 small onion, roughly chopped
1 tablespoon unsalted butter
4 garlic cloves, finely chopped

2 tablespoons all-purpose flour
1 cup chicken stock
½ teaspoon salt
½ teaspoon ground black pepper
½ teaspoon each chopped sage and
    thyme leaves

Piecrust:
2⅔ cups all-purpose flour, plus extra
    for dusting
½ teaspoon kosher salt
¼ teaspoon ground cinnamon
¼ teaspoon ground nutmeg
2 sticks (1 cup) unsalted butter,
    frozen and cut into ½-inch cubes
milk, for brushing

Heat the oven to 350°F. Lightly grease a square 9-inch baking dish suitable to serve from. To make the piecrust, sift the flour, salt and spices into a large mixing bowl, then cut the butter into the flour with a knife until the mixture resembles coarse bread crumbs. Gradually add 3 to 5 tablespoons water, mixing with a fork and then your hands until it forms a ball of dough. Halve the dough and roll each piece out on a lightly floured work surface to ½ inch thick. Line the bottom and sides of the dish with half the dough. Put the other piece of dough on a board lined with wax paper. Chill both while you make the filling.

Heat the oil in a large saucepan over medium heat. Add the chicken and sear until brown on both sides. Remove the chicken from the pan, then cut it into chunks and put in a mixing bowl. Leave to one side. Reduce the heat to medium-low. Add the carrots, celery, potatoes, peas and half the onion to the pan and cook until just soft, then add to the chicken.

Melt the butter in the same pan over medium heat. Add the remaining onion and the garlic and cook 5 to 8 minutes until the onion begins to brown. Stir in the flour, then add the chicken stock, salt, pepper and herbs and cook, stirring until the mixture thickens. Pour it over the chicken and vegetables, then leave to cool completely.

When cold, pour the mixture into the dough-lined dish. Top with the remaining dough and pinch the edges together to seal. Brush with milk and cut a few slits in the top. Bake 30 to 40 minutes, until the pastry is golden. Leave to stand 5 minutes before serving.

CAPE COD CLAM CHOWDER

This is the way my mother would make chowder for us when there were plenty of clams to use up. Alternatively, she would use mussels, which also worked really well. This soup is simple, but deliciously comforting on a cold winter's evening, and you can jazz it up, as my mom used to do, by adding a little saffron or other spices to the mix.

Serves 4 to 6
Preparation time: 30 minutes
Cooking time: 1 hour 20 minutes

6½ pounds clams
fish stock or bottled clam juice,
 as needed
4 ounces bacon

2 onions, chopped
2 large potatoes, peeled and diced
2 cups plus 2 tablespoons heavy
 cream
kosher salt and freshly ground
 black pepper
snipped chives, to serve

Scrub the clams thoroughly with a stiff brush under cold running water to remove all traces of grit. Rinse and discard any with broken shells or that do not close as soon as they are tapped.

Put the clams in a large saucepan (or use 2 saucepans, if necessary) with a splash of water over medium heat, cover with a tight-fitting lid and steam 8 minutes, shaking the pan occasionally, or until the shells open. Discard any that remain closed. Drain the clams, reserving any liquid.

Cool the clams slightly, then remove all the meat from the shells and leave to one side. Strain the cooking liquid through a strainer into a heatproof pitcher, making it up to 2½ cups with fish stock or bottled clam juice and leave to one side.

Heat a skillet over medium heat. Fry the bacon until crisp, then drain on paper towels and leave to one side. Add the onions to the fat in the pan and cook over medium heat 5 minutes, or until soft and translucent. Transfer the onions to a large saucepan, stir in the clam cooking liquid and add the potatoes. Bring to a boil, then boil 5 minutes, stirring occasionally. Reduce the heat to low, then simmer 25 minutes, or until the potatoes are tender and falling apart. Stir in the cream and simmer 15 minutes longer.

Meanwhile, chop the bacon, then add the clams and half the bacon to the chowder and cook 5 minutes, or until thoroughly heated through. Season with salt and pepper, then serve sprinkled with the remaining bacon and the chives.

BROWN BETTY

I have adapted this from one of my mother's recipes, which originated from her much-used copy of *The Pennsylvania Dutch Cookbook*, published by the Culinary Arts Press in 1936. My mother, who hated waste, would make it using apples that were a bit old and soft, carefully cutting out any brown bits.

Serves 4
Preparation time: 20 minutes
Cooking time: 35 minutes

4 tablespoons unsalted butter
4 apples, peeled, cored and thinly
    sliced

6 slices of brown bread, roughly
    crumbled
6 tablespoons soft brown sugar
¼ teaspoon ground cinnamon
⅛ teaspoon freshly grated nutmeg
vanilla ice cream, to serve

Heat the oven to 350°F and grease the bottom of a deep baking dish that is suitable to serve from with one-third of the butter. Arrange one-third of the apples in an even layer on the bottom of the dish, then top with a layer of bread crumbs and half the sugar. Sprinkle lightly with about half the cinnamon and nutmeg.

Add another layer of apples, the remaining bread crumbs, half the remaining sugar and spices. Dot with half the remaining butter and add the rest of the apples.

Cover with the remaining sugar, then sprinkle with the remaining cinnamon and nutmeg. Dot with the rest of the butter, then spoon 6 tablespoons hot water over.

Cover the dish loosely with foil and bake 30 minutes. Meanwhile, heat the broiler to medium-high. Remove the foil and broil 5 minutes until the topping is brown. Serve with vanilla ice cream.

BLACK CHERRY CREAM PIE

My mother's favorite recipe book was *The Mystery Chef's Own Cook Book*, written by John MacPherson, the famous radio cook she used to listen to when she lived in New York. This is my own adaptation of a family favorite from that marvelously quirky book.

Serves 4
Preparation time: 40 minutes, plus cooling
Cooking time: 15 minutes

1 pound black cherries
5 tablespoons sugar
1½ tablespoons cornstarch
1 cup whipping cream

Piecrust:
1¼ sticks (10 tablespoons) chilled unsalted butter, cubed, plus extra for greasing
1¾ cups all-purpose flour, plus extra for dusting
1 teaspoon baking powder
1 tablespoon sugar
⅛ teaspoon salt

Heat the oven to 425°F. Grease a deep 8-inch tart pan with butter. To make the piecrust, sift the flour and baking powder into a large mixing bowl, then stir in the sugar and salt. Add the butter and rub it in with your fingertips until the mixture resembles fine bread crumbs. Stir in 1 tablespoon cold water and gently knead together to form a ball of dough, adding more water if necessary. Do not overknead the dough or the baked pastry will be heavy.

Roll out the dough on a lightly floured work surface into a circle 2 inches larger than the tart pan, then use to line the bottom and side of the prepared pan. Fold any extra dough back over the edge and crimp it all the way around with your fingers and thumb to make a thick border. Prick the bottom and side of the dough with a fork. Line with wax paper and fill with rice or baking beans. Bake 15 minutes, then remove the paper and beans and bake 10 minutes longer, or until the pastry is golden and crisp. Leave to cool completely.

Meanwhile, put the cherries, sugar and ⅔ cup water in a saucepan and simmer until they are soft. Strain the cherries, reserving the juice, then leave to cool. Once cooled, remove all the cherry pits and leave the cherries to one side; discard the pits.

Mix the cornstarch with 3 tablespoons cold water in a small bowl until smooth, then stir it into the reserved cherry juice. Pour into a saucepan and simmer gently until it thickens into a syrup, then add the pitted cherries and mix together. Leave to cool completely.

Whip the cream until soft peaks form. Pile the cream into the cooled pastry case, then top with the cherries and syrup before serving.

*From left pictured front, Sforzino and Fiammetta
with two of their Sforza uncles.*

11. *Montignoso*
UNDER GERMAN OCCUPATION

It was not only my grandfather's family that was persecuted by the Fascists in Italy. Carlo and Valentine had managed to escape to America with their children, but other members of the Sforza family did not fare so well. Carlo's brothers, Cesare and Alessandro, stayed behind in the little village of Montignoso, in the Apuan Alps, where both of them suffered terribly under German occupation. News of their plight occasionally filtered through, but there was little Carlo or the rest of his family could do, except hope and pray that one day it would all be over.

Among the many family documents I have been left, I found Alessandro's journal. I find it very hard to read; and almost impossible not to. In it, Carlo's brother describes vividly the terrible atmosphere of suspicion and mistrust that surrounded his family during the Fascist years. His family home was under surveillance or attack constantly, the walls peppered with bullet holes —mostly around his bedroom window. The entire Sforza family had become a target of the Fascists: Carlo's house was torched by the Blackshirts; Cesare was arrested; and their other brother Ascanio was heavily involved in the fight against fascism.

Day after day, they were met with harassment from the locals. Their enemies' main objective seemed to be a relentless, systematic besmirching of the Sforza name. In this, their own ancestral land, vicious gossip about the family spread like wild fire, mainly put about by the women of La Spezia. These wives and girlfriends of absent sailors and artillerymen, who ran the tightest black-market businesses, had moved up into the mountains, away from the worst of the bombing. They told the Germans—and anybody else who cared to listen—a radio was often heard transmitting in English from inside the Sforza house and the family were traitors and renegades.

> **The entire Sforza family had become a target of the Fascists: Carlo's house was torched by the Blackshirts...**

Food was scarce, especially during the winter months, and there were many mouths to feed. The cook did her best to keep food on the table, even if it was only a thick bean and vegetable soup, the bowl lined with thick slices of stale bread to make the soup even more filling. Chestnut flour, which had for centuries been a valuable source of starch in these mountains, now became invaluable, and was used to make a kind of thin gruel. Sometimes it was all there was to eat for several days at a time, but the cook occasionally managed to make it more palatable with the addition of a handful of mushrooms, a sausage or cheese rind. With wheat flour impossible to get hold of, chestnut flour was used to make bread. Everything the family and servants could forage they did, and they managed to find some passable substitutes for everyday foods. They gathered wild, blue-flowered chicory, roasting and grinding its roots to make coffee. There was precious little food stored away for long hard times such as these.

One spring day, sick of being confined to his house by the German guards who had watched over his every move throughout the winter, Alessandro bravely took his wife and children for a walk through his fields and olive groves in the warm sunshine. On the way back, as they came round a bend in the lane, he was surprised to see a car parked in the road with its door open. A very pretty, well-dressed Italian woman leaned out and called out to him, "Oh hello! We've heard so much about you and your lovely house. What a beautiful place! We want to help you. Please, get in the car—it will be quicker that way. We need to give you a very important envelope!"

A little warily, Alessandro got into the car, leaving his wife and children standing in the lane. There were three passengers inside, all of whom were charming—chatting innocuously and paying him compliments. I do not know if Alessandro sensed something was not quite right, but he soon realized he was in trouble: at the crossroads, instead of turning right, toward the house, the car turned left and accelerated away, very fast, toward Viareggio. When Alessandro remarked that they had turned the wrong way, the woman snarled at him, "The SS is arresting you."

Alessandro was taken to the Murate prison, in Florence, where he was beaten, starved and denied any small comfort or medical assistance. It took his wife, Maria, two days to reach the prison on foot, but they were only allowed nine precious minutes together before she was told to leave. She had brought him food and warm clothes, but he was not allowed to keep them.

Top, Uncle Cesare with
family members.
Right, the grape harvest at
Montignoso with Fiammetta
and Sforzino.

Things got worse for Alessandro when, in the dead of night, he was moved to the prison of the Torre di San Leonardo, in Verona, where he remained until the following April. His damp, dark, suffocating cave of a cell—number 40—measured just four by four meters, and housed eight inmates. The atrocities he witnessed during his incarceration were horrendous, but he was freed eventually, after which he escaped with his family over the border, north of Turin. The last line of my great-uncle's journal reads: "Free Switzerland welcomes us, and saves us."

> ## The last line of my great-uncle's journal reads: "Free Switzerland welcomes us, and saves us."

The faded, yellow pages of my great-uncle's journal are painful to read, and what you have here is only a very short, potted version of the whole story. Although I never met Alessandro or Cesare, I know most of the people involved, and their children, my cousins. I know Carlo found his family's plight extremely hard to bear; forced into exile he had to leave them all behind, to be persecuted ruthlessly for standing against the Fascist regime. I often think of Alessandro's struggling family in Montignoso, surviving on what they could forage, when I cook one of the classic Italian *la cucina povera* dishes. Here are some of the wartime recipes that somehow managed to nourish them through those terrible, dark times.

Pictured from left: Uncle Cesare, Fiammetta, Nonno Carlo and other Sforza family members in the Apuan Alps.

POLENTA WITH SAUSAGES & BEANS

Beppino could never make this dish without telling me about his wartime hardships, some of which were truly unimaginable. Dry beans, soaked overnight and then cooked (see page 96), can be used instead of canned, if you like, and you can add a handful of grated Parmesan cheese to the polenta to make it even more filling and flavorsome.

Serves 6
Preparation time: 15 minutes
Cooking time: about 1 hour

2 tablespoons vegetable oil
2 garlic cloves, chopped
1 onion, chopped
1 celery stick, chopped
1 carrot, chopped
2 teaspoons chopped parsley leaves

12 Italian link sausages
1 tablespoon tomato paste
1 can (15-oz.) borlotti beans, drained
  and rinsed
1½ cups vegetable stock
2 cups fine, medium or coarse polenta
kosher salt and freshly ground
  black pepper

Heat the oil in a large, heavy-based saucepan over medium heat. Add the garlic, onion, celery, carrot and parsley and fry 5 to 10 minutes until the vegetables are soft. Add the sausages and fry for a few minutes until light brown all over.

Mix together the tomato paste and 4 tablespoons water, then add to the pan. Stir well, then add the beans and vegetable stock, season with salt and pepper and bring to a boil. Reduce the heat to low, cover the pan and simmer 45 minutes, adding more water if necessary, until the sauce is thick and the sausages are cooked through.

Meanwhile, cook the polenta. Pour 7½ cups water into a wide, heavy-based, preferably copper, pan and bring to a boil over high heat. Trickle the polenta into the boiling water in a fine stream, whisking continuously. When all the polenta has been added, reduce the heat to medium-low and continue to stir with a strong, long-handled wooden spoon until the polenta comes away from the side of the pan. This takes about 50 minutes and requires a strong elbow.

Turn the polenta out onto a wooden board and smooth it into a mound with a spatula. Leave it to stand 5 minutes, covered with a clean dish towel. Cut the polenta into wedges and serve hot with the sausage and bean sauce spooned over the top.

BAKED MACKEREL FILLETS

My mother told me this was one of those wartime recipes made when bread was available, as the crumbs were liberally added to bulk out the other ingredients. Ask your fish merchant to fillet the mackerel for you—you need large, neat, flat fillets you can sandwich the filling between.

Serves 4
Preparation time: 20 minutes
Cooking time: 15 minutes

2 tablespoons extra virgin olive oil
8 mackerel fillets, about 18 ounces
   total weight, dressed and trimmed
2 tablespoons dry white wine or water
green salad, to serve (optional)

Filling:
4 tablespoons fresh white
   bread crumbs

1 heaped tablespoons salted capers,
   rinsed, drained and chopped
3 large salted anchovy fillets, rinsed,
   drained and chopped
2 garlic cloves, finely chopped
2 tablespoons chopped parsley leaves
1 tablespoon pine nuts, chopped
2 tablespoons freshly grated Parmesan
   or Pecorino cheese
2 tablespoons extra virgin olive oil
kosher salt and freshly ground
   black pepper

Heat the oven to 375°F and grease a baking dish, large enough for the mackerel "sandwiches" to sit snugly, with half the oil.

Put all the filling ingredients in a bowl and mix together well, then season with pepper. You are unlikely to need salt as the anchovies are very salty.

Lay half the fish fillets, skin side down, on a cutting board and spoon about 1 heaped tablespoon of the filling over each. Top with the remaining fillets, flesh side down, pressing down firmly to secure.

Transfer the mackerel "sandwiches" to the greased dish, sprinkling any remaining filling over the fish. Drizzle the remaining oil over and sprinkle lightly with the wine. Bake on the top shelf of the oven 15 minutes, or until cooked through, then leave to rest 3 minutes. Serve the baked mackerel with a green salad, if liked.

BREAD & TOMATO SOUP

In times of hardship, my family has always been good at using their imagination (and any available ingredients) to make a meal full of flavor and nourishing to eat. In our house, this soup was revered as one of those dishes that kept morale buoyant in one of the hardest moments of my family's history.

Serves 4
Preparation time: 30 minutes,
  plus cooling
Cooking time: about 3 hours

½ cup olive oil
1 onion, chopped
7 cups roughly chopped very ripe,
  soft tomatoes
14 ounces stale bread, crusts removed
  and thinly sliced
3 garlic cloves, crushed
1 handful of basil leaves, chopped,
  plus extra torn leaves, to serve
kosher salt and freshly ground
  black pepper

Vegetable broth:
3 carrots, scraped and quartered
2 onions, halved
3 celery sticks, quartered
3 tomatoes, halved (optional)
2 zucchini, cut into large chunks
3 cabbage leaves, quartered
1 small leek, rinsed, trimmed and
  halved
12 lettuce leaves, halved
3 pinches of salt

First, make the broth. Put all the vegetables in a large saucepan or stockpot, add the salt and pour in 8¾ cups water. Bring to a boil gently over low heat, then cover and simmer 1½ hours. Remove the pan from the heat and leave the broth to cool completely. Strain through a fine strainer into a bowl or large pitcher and discard the vegetables. If not using immediately, chill the broth, covered, up to 3 days or freeze up to 3 months.

To make the soup, pour 1½ quarts of the strained broth into a large saucepan and heat gently until hot.

Meanwhile, heat half the oil in a saucepan over low heat. Add the onion and tomatoes and fry 10 minutes, stirring regularly, until soft. Push the mixture through a food mill or strainer, then add it to the hot broth.

Add the bread, garlic and basil, then season with salt and pepper. Cover and simmer gently 45 minutes, stirring occasionally, or until thick and creamy. Stir in the remaining oil and add a little more salt and pepper, if you like. Serve the soup sprinkled with torn basil leaves.

CHESTNUT FLOUR CAKE

During wartime, the chestnuts harvested for centuries on the Apuan Alps saved many of the local population, including my own family members, from outright starvation. The chestnuts were dried and ground and then used to make wheat flour go farther in bread, pasta and many other dishes. There is no rising agent in this cake; it is supposed to be quite dense and slightly elastic, and the texture varies according to whether it is baked in a deep cake pan or a wide, shallow baking tray.

Serves 6
Preparation time: 30 minutes,
  plus 30 minutes standing
Cooking time: 35 to 45 minutes

6 tablespoons extra virgin olive oil
3½ cups chestnut flour, sifted
6 tablespoons sugar

a pinch of salt
⅔ cup golden raisins
2 tablespoons rosemary leaves
  or fennel seeds
grated zest of 1 orange
⅓ cup pine nuts

Grease a deep 8-inch cake pan or shallow baking tray (see above) with 3 tablespoons of the oil and leave to one side. Mix together the chestnut flour, sugar and salt in a large bowl, then whisk in as much of the remaining oil as you like—the more you add, the oilier the final consistency of the cake. Gradually add 4½ cups water, whisking continuously to make a thick, lump-free batter. Leave to stand 30 minutes.

Meanwhile, heat the oven to 375°F. Soak the sultanas in warm water for 10 minutes, then drain and pat dry with paper towels.

Mix the batter again, then pour it into the prepared pan or tray and level the surface with a spatula. Sprinkle with the rosemary or fennel seeds, orange zest, soaked sultanas and pine nuts. Bake 35 to 45 minutes, depending on how dry or moist you like your cake. The tip of a knife inserted into the cake should come out clean. Serve warm or at room temperature, cut into slices or wedges.

My mother, Fiammetta, and Nonna Valentine.

12. THE RETURN TO ITALY VIA THE SPICE-SCENTED PORT OF *Casablanca*

In 1944, my mother and grandmother returned from their three years of exile in the United States on a US army ship, via the Port of Casablanca, in North Africa. Fiammetta was twenty-nine. She was feeling enormously homesick for Italy, despite having enjoyed her American adventure, her time in New York in particular. Her father had never let her stop feeling for Italy during their many years of exile and her whole being ached for the country she loved. She told me often how the thought of being back on Italian soil had kept her from sleeping during the entire voyage home.

Carlo, eager to get back into frontline politics as quickly as possible, had set off for England with his son, Sforzino, several months earlier on one of the rare transatlantic flights. One of the first things he did once he had landed in the United Kingdom was to meet with Winston Churchill for some rather frank and explosive discussions. Carlo still felt keenly that his warnings about the dangers of Mussolini's leadership and its potential outcomes should have been heeded by Churchill before the war, who had instead turned a deaf ear to them.

Fiammetta and Valentine followed by ship, having packed up their belongings and said goodbye to all the good friends they had made. It was time to go home at last. The ship was filled with GIs, on their way to liberate Italy. Mostly, these were men who had never been outside their own home state, let alone the country. They were overexcited at being on the ship and a part of the war. My mother told me that it was on this voyage that she first properly awoke to a wider sexual understanding. She had never been exposed to the kind of exhibitionism these boys adopted, partly to cover up their terror of war. She sat watching them, quietly knitting a jumper to keep her hands busy, while her emotions ran high.

> One of the first things he did... in the UK was to meet with Winston Churchill for some rather frank and explosive discussions.

Their first stop, once safely across the Atlantic, was the port of Casablanca. Having eaten a Moroccan dinner of spicy bean soup, chicken tagine and lamb and date stew accompanied by a mountain of cinnamon-scented couscous, Fiammetta settled her mother in her room with a tray of mint tea and a little dish of almond sweetmeats. She went downstairs to the hotel foyer, too excited to sleep. Italy was just across the water and she could not wait to breathe the air of home once again. The heat was oppressive and the GIs noisy. She sat in a corner with her knitting, watching them cavort with the local women, who looked exotic in their Moroccan clothes. She sat there deep into the night as they came and went. There appeared to be no end of available women and the young men seemed to her impossibly far away from their squeaky clean all-American homes, wrapped in their brown, bangle-covered arms.

At about 3 o'clock in the morning, a timid Italian man approached Fiammetta and sat down beside her.

"Are you the Contessina Sforza?" he whispered. "On your way home?"

"*Si*," she replied, continuing to knit.

"Please come with me, Contessina," he begged. "There is something you can do for your country right away. We need you."

In hindsight, Fiammetta realized it had been very risky to believe this man and let him lead her away, but that is exactly what happened. In the back of a jeep, with no headlights to light their way through the dark streets of wartime Casablanca, my mother lurched around, hanging on for dear life. She did not know where she was going, though in her heart she was certain that she was meant to be there, and that she was destined to help her countrymen. Out into the desert night they went, on and on until they came upon a fenced-in area about the size of a football field, next to a few basic huts.

The driver of the jeep signaled just once with his torch and they got out. My mother walked with him across the cold sand in the dark until they were up against the fence of the compound. On the other side, a hundred or more Italian prisoners of war emerged from out of the darkness, whispering to Fiammetta and slipping tiny bits of paper into her hands.

"Please let my family know I'm alive."

"Please Contessina, tell my mother I am safe."

"Contessina, tell my children I love them."

Right, my dad—
the handsome devil!
Below, my mom falling
in love with my dad.

Fiammetta took the scraps of paper and, touching the outstretched hands through the wire fence, she promised the parents, sons, daughters, wives, husbands, brothers, sisters and nonni that she would do everything she possibly could to pass on their messages as soon as she was back in Italy.

Then there was a sudden movement over by the huts and a flash of light from another torch. Fiammetta's companion quickly pulled her away from the fence and thrust her into the jeep. Moments later they were on their way back, my mother's hands filled with scraps of paper covered in tiny writing. Neither the driver nor Fiammetta spoke a single word on their journey. She never knew his name or heard from him again.

It was wonderful to be home and to be among their friends and family, but Italy was in a dreadful state...

As soon as Fiammetta was safely back in her hotel room she unraveled her knitting wool and rewound it around the little bits of paper. She was sure her luggage would be searched repeatedly on their way home and it was the only place she could think of hiding them. During the rest of the voyage her mind was whirling: how was she going to track down these people's families and not break her promises? Her knitting, buried at the bottom of her belongings, remained untouched, the secrets inside the ball of yarn kept safe.

The following evening, the ship docked in Naples and mother and daughter traveled on to Rome, where they were finally reunited with Carlo and Sforzino. It was wonderful to be home and to be among their family and friends, but Italy was in a dreadful state at the end of the war and there was much to do. As soon as the family was settled, Fiammetta set out to find those people whose addresses were hidden in her knitting wool. And so began her personal and extraordinary mission that was to lead to her meeting the love of her life—my father.

On her forays into the countryside outside Rome, Fiammetta always took along a willing GI who would have no complaints about spending his day off with a beautiful girl who spoke Italian and English so perfectly. Together, they sought out lost children—orphaned or abandoned by their parents—many of whom were sheltering in the ruins of their homes alone and living, quite literally, off the land. My mother found many young children, damaged by their experiences of war. She would load them into the truck and take them home to her parents' house. She scrubbed and washed them, cuddled and fed them as best she could. Some of them—those who had wintered outside for more than one season—had developed a natural gray down all over their bodies. It was a simple gift from Mother Nature, to protect them from the cold, my mother told me: "It just went away after the third bath." Fiammetta would care for these children's physical wounds and then try to find them a new home.

"In the end," she told me, "I persuaded some of the Yanks to adopt them. Many of the children went to live in the States. They still write sometimes, and some of their children, too."

My mother never forgot those Italian voices that asked for her help in the desert. Her quest to find the relatives of the prisoners of war she had met in Casablanca led her to seek help from the Office for War Information. It was there that she met my father, Howard, whose job it was to to reunite all those families that had been displaced and torn apart by the war. The spark between my parents was ignited at a New Year's Eve party on December 31, 1944.

My dad.

CHICKEN TAGINE WITH PRESERVED LEMON & OLIVES

This lovely, tangy, rich chicken dish is very typical of the best kind of Moroccan cooking. My mother used to make this in an old clay tagine, and served it on top of a pile of fluffy couscous, steamed over a pan of simmering chicken stock.

Serves 4 to 6
Preparation time: 30 minutes,
   plus 1 hour marinating
Cooking time: about 1 hour

3 to 4 pounds chicken leg and thigh
   pieces
1 large preserved lemon
2 tablespoons olive oil
3 garlic cloves, finely chopped
1 onion, chopped
½ cup mixed olives, pitted
¼ cup raisins
3 tablespoons chopped cilantro leaves

3 tablespoons chopped parsley leaves
kosher salt
steamed couscous, to serve

Spice mix:
2 teaspoons paprika
1 teaspoon ground cumin
1 teaspoon ground ginger
1 teaspoon turmeric
½ teaspoon ground cinnamon
¼ teaspoon freshly ground black
   pepper

Combine all the spice mix ingredients in a large bowl. Pat the chicken pieces dry with paper towels and add to the bowl, then turn to coat them in the spice mixture. Cover and leave to marinate in the refrigerator 1 hour.

Meanwhile, rinse the preserved lemon, then remove the peel and discard the pulp. Cut the peel into thin strips and leave to one side.

Heat the oil in a large, heavy-based saucepan over medium-high heat. Add the chicken pieces, skin side down, sprinkle lightly with salt and fry 5 minutes, or until brown all over. (If you are using a clay tagine, put on a diffuser over medium heat to prevent the tagine from cracking. Do not brown the chicken, but add with the oil, garlic and onion and continue as detailed below.) Reduce the heat to medium-low and add the garlic and onion, then cover and cook 15 minutes, or until the onion is soft.

Turn the chicken pieces over, then add generous ⅓ cup water and the preserved lemon peel, olives and raisins. Reduce the heat to low, cover and cook 30 to 40 minutes longer, adding more water, if necessary, until the chicken is tender and the juices run clear when the meat is pierced with the tip of a sharp knife. Stir in the herbs, season and serve with couscous.

CASABLANCA LAMB & DATE STEW

My mother always loved dates and we often had them in the house when I was growing up, and not just at Christmas time when they are traditionally most popular. This was one of my mother's favorite lamb dishes and one which I think must have always reminded her of stopping off in Casablanca during that long voyage back from the United States on her way home to Italy.

Serves 4
Preparation time: 20 minutes
Cooking time: 45 minutes

1 tablespoon olive oil
1 onion, finely chopped
1 pound 2 ounces boneless lamb leg, trimmed of fat and cubed
2 cups peeled and cubed sweet potatoes
2 teaspoons ground coriander

2 teaspoons ground cinnamon
¼ teaspoon ground mild chili
juice of 2 clementines
1 tablespoon tomato paste
⅓ cup dates, pitted
2 tablespoons finely chopped cilantro leaves
1 tablespoon finely grated unwaxed clementine zest
steamed couscous or rice, to serve

Heat the oil in a large, heavy-based saucepan over high heat. Add the onion and lamb and fry until the lamb is light brown all over, turning frequently. Add the sweet potatoes and spices and mix well.

Add 2 cups just-boiled water, the clementine juice and tomato paste and stir well, then bring to a boil and cook 3 minutes. Reduce the heat to low, cover and simmer 20 minutes, or until the sweet potatoes and lamb are tender. Remove the lid, stir in the dates and simmer 10 minutes longer, or until the dates are soft and the sauce reduces and is thick.

Scatter the cilantro and clementine zest over the stew, then serve with steamed couscous or rice.

MOROCCAN SPICY BEAN SOUP

A wonderful winter warmer, this is one of those invigorating, almost spine-tingling, soups that also manages to be really satisfying. My mother loved to make this, although she did not use as much harissa as I do. I'm sure it was inspired by the brief time she spent in Casablanca on that arduous journey home. Dry beans, soaked overnight and then cooked (see page 96), can be used instead of canned, if you like. You need to halve the quantity of beans if using dry rather than canned.

Serves 4 to 6
Preparation time: 10 minutes
Cooking time: 45 minutes

6 ripe tomatoes
½ can (15-oz.) navy or cannellini
  beans, drained and rinsed
½ can (15-oz.) chickpeas, drained and
  rinsed
½ can (15-oz.) borlotti or pinto beans,
  drained and rinsed

1 large onion, finely chopped
2 tablespoons lemon juice
1 teaspoon ground cumin
1 teaspoon turmeric
¼ cup long-grain rice
2 tablespoons chopped cilantro
  leaves, plus extra to serve
2 teaspoons harissa paste
kosher salt and freshly ground
  black pepper

Cut a cross in the bottom of each tomato, using a sharp knife, then put them in a heatproof bowl and cover with just-boiled water. Leave to stand 2 to 3 minutes, then drain. Peel off and discard the skins, then seed and roughly chop the flesh.

Put all the beans in a large saucepan with the onion, tomatoes, lemon juice and spices. Add 7½ cups water and bring to a boil, then reduce the heat, cover and simmer 30 minutes.

Stir in the rice and simmer 12 minutes longer, or until the rice is tender. Stir in the cilantro and harissa, then season with salt and pepper to taste. Serve the soup topped with extra cilantro.

MOROCCAN CARROT, ORANGE & RADISH SALAD

I love this salad, which is a great way to use both carrots and radishes, and, like my mother, I love using orange-flower water, with its amazingly elusive flavor. I have always associated oranges with North Africa, Morocco in particular, as they have a special sweetness there that is very unique. Orange blossoms will always remind me of my mother, and the story she told me of her wedding day and the gift she received from her cousin Giovannino Sforza of a dachshund puppy, sitting in a box filled with orange blossom!

Serves 4
Preparation time: 15 minutes

4 cups peeled and grated carots
2 oranges, peeled and segmented
1 large onion, diced
4 large radishes, thinly sliced
2 tablespoons chopped cilantro
  leaves, to serve
warm pita bread, to serve

Dressing:
3 tablespoons olive oil
2 tablespoons lemon juice
2 tablespoons orange juice
2 teaspoons orange-flower water
1 teaspoon ground cinnamon
2 tablespoons chopped cilantro leaves
kosher salt and freshly ground
  black pepper

Combine the carrots, oranges, onion and radishes in a salad bowl.

To make the dressing, whisk together the olive oil, lemon and orange juice, orange-flower water and cinnamon. Season with salt and pepper and continue to whisk the dressing until it is slightly thick. Stir in the chopped cilantro.

Pour the dressing over the salad. Toss everything together, then cover and chill until ready to serve. Toss with the cilantro leaves and serve with warm pita bread.

*My mother and father's wedding day at the
Campidoglio, Rome, 1946.*

13. *Mamma* AND DAD:
THEIR SCANDALOUS MARRIAGE

In 1946, my mother Fiammetta was excommunicated from the Roman Catholic Church because she married my father. This might explain many things about my upbringing and my rather jaded view of organized religion. But it probably says more about love in general.

My father, Howard Scott, was a fine, upstanding British army officer. He was divorced with two children: my half-brother and -sister, Gerard and Angela. He was also penniless, having lost his business when it was destroyed in the blitzkrieg. Before the war, his small advertising agency had done well: my father was proud of having been instrumental in introducing Kellogg's Corn Flakes to Britain, via teams of hawkers who posted small wrapped boxes of the cereal through the mailboxes of homes in London, Birmingham and Manchester. I have a faded photograph somewhere that shows a team of my dad's hawkers whitewashing the kerb of a pavement to indicate that they had just finished delivering the boxes to every household on the street.

My parents met on New Year's Eve 1944, at a huge party in Rome. For reasons I have never quite understood—because neither of them ever really explained it properly—both of them were there on some obscure-yet-official spying mission. When they came face to face, my father said, "What are you doing here? You shouldn't be here!" at precisely the same moment my mother said the same. Presumably there was a reason and it was explained, but I like to believe that they were both there because destiny had somehow decreed that they should meet and fall in love.

Soon after, my father was posted to Trieste, during which time my mother worked for the Red Cross in Rome. Often, Howard would steal his colonel's car and drive through the night on a tank or two of ethanol to spend just a few precious hours with Fiammetta. They wrote endless letters to each other during this period, all of which I have kept. Filled with little snippets of everyday news, the

> Howard would steal his colonel's car and drive through the night... to spend just a few precious hours with Fiammetta.

pages show their passion for one another that seemed to deepen, letter by letter. They had secret nicknames for one another and I have always read their letters with a slight sense of guilt; I feel I am trespassing on something very private and very deep.

Fiammetta's family and friends, as well as Carlo's political colleagues, were up in arms about this union. After everything that the family had been through, the last thing anybody expected was that my mother should fall for an Englishman, and such an unsuitable one at that. Not only was he not an Italian, a Catholic or an aristocrat, but he had been married before.

When they could get away from their work, Howard and Fiammetta loved to spend time near the sea, especially in places like the little harbor of Lerici, on the border between Tuscany and Liguria. People used to travel for miles to eat the catch of the day, and my parents loved the freshly netted silver-blue, shiny anchovies, cooked in all manner of styles; or the great bowls of the salty-sweet *zuppa di datteri di mare*, those narrow mussel-like creatures that burrow their way deep inside rocks, whose lovely latin name is *Lithophaga lithophaga*. (They can no longer be caught, because the harvesting of them became illegal in 1988.)

Many years later, my father and I would also spend hours together in Lerici, eating ice cream and talking about classical music. Wandering around the cool, narrow backstreets, we would sometimes discover that some of the same little trattorie were still there. Except for a slightly wider choice of dishes on the menu, little else appeared to have changed in the course of the two-and-a-half decades since my courting parents had eaten at their tables.

In those early postwar times of their courtship, there was never much choice on the menu, but my parents discovered a mutual appreciation of gastronomy as they ate the freshly caught fish and slices of fruit with a glass of white wine. My father would always say my mother had a razor-sharp instinct when it came to ordering the best dishes on the menu. My mother would laugh at this: "Whatever he ordered, he'd always prefer the food on my plate, even though he always refused to order the same thing as me. He'd get so cross with himself!" My father, remembering those days, would chuckle and kiss her: "Yes, but you were always prepared to share with me!"

My parents' love, immense and all-consuming, never waned: even when they were very old and my father was so terribly ill, they would hold hands on the sofa like young lovers. Food was especially important then: my mother

My mom and dad in the Cinque Terre.

understood—even through the demented tempests in the last few years of his life, when communication with my father became distorted in so many ways —that food was the one true enjoyment he had left. She would spend hours cooking all his favorite dishes: tender, juicy broiled steaks; perfect pan-fried trout scattered with toasted almonds; or velvety smooth vegetable soups. She would set the table every breakfast, lunch and dinner with great care, making sure everything he ate was as mouthwateringly wonderful as possible.

My father was not an easy man. He was demanding, belligerent and determined. He did not suffer fools gladly and had a fiery temper when aroused. One thing that inflamed his wrath was when any of us were late for lunch or dinner. Mealtimes were sacred. Being late would result in fierce punishments and even my mother, who sometimes returned late from the hairdressers or a visit to a friend, would walk into a terrible storm of rage.

"Stop it," she would say to him firmly. "You're behaving like your father! I'm here now. Please, let's just eat." And so the meal would begin, silently, with my father still obviously fuming, so much so it was hard for him to swallow the food. We would eat in a rush, keen for the meal to end so we could scatter and leave our parents to make their peace. In restaurants, though, it was worse: it was horribly embarrassing when Dad made a scene. I have witnessed more than one overturned table because we had been kept waiting for our order longer than he felt was permissible.

If I refused to eat something at the table, my father would have it removed and there would be nothing except bread offered in exchange. The refused dish would then be presented to me at every meal for several days, until I cracked and attempted to eat it, at which point he would have it removed and I was allowed to eat what everybody else was having. I could never meet my mother's eye during these episodes because she would always wink at me, which would make me laugh, and that would infuriate my father even more. He never let on he knew about the wedges of crumbly, salty cheese and sweet ripe pears my mother would sneak up to my room at night after I had gone to bed hungry, but I somehow suspect he did.

My father knew it was very important for my grandmother Valentine that his and Fiammetta's marriage should be celebrated in church, preferably a Roman Catholic one, so he tried very hard to make this happen. An audience with a Cardinal, influential in the Vatican City, was arranged, but when my father asked if they could at least be permitted a simple church blessing he was told that it was not possible. A visit to England, to the Archbishop of Canterbury's advisors, also proved fruitless. The facts were these: Fiammetta and Howard could not be married or blessed in a church because my father had been married before, and had two children to prove it. So they had no choice but to be married at the Campidoglio, in a civil ceremony, attended by a couple of cousins and a few friends. Significantly, neither Valentine nor my uncle Sforzino attended, but Carlo was there—a strong, solid presence at his daughter's side.

Carlo stepped out of the political arena after the scandal of my mother's marriage, due to ill-health. His closest allies within the government had said to him: "Carlo, you can become Italy's first postwar prime minister and rebuild your country, but only if your daughter does not marry that Englishman." My Nonno was having none of it, and replied with this simple sentence: "What matters now is my daughter's happiness."

After the wedding in Rome, my Nonno arranged for Howard and Fiammetta to live on the shores of Lake Como, in the wing of a crumbling palazzo that belonged to a friend of the family. There they were to lie low for a few months until the scandal of their marriage had died down. Exactly a year later, on July 10, 1947, my brother Steve was born in Milan. During that period and for a couple of years afterward, my mother spent a great deal of her time alone, bringing up her sons (Nick was born just over a year later). Howard had set them up in a house in the Lombardy countryside, called La Canonica, while he worked hard in the city to start up the new postwar family business: schools teaching English as a foreign language. All my mother's best pieces of inherited jewelry were sold to provide the seed capital for the enterprise.

Once the gossips had turned their focus to somebody new, and ruffled family feelings had been calmed by the passage of time, Carlo gave my parents La Tambura, the house in Tuscany, as a belated wedding gift. It was there that Fiammetta began to create a real home. And even though my family lived in Milan, and then in Rome for a long time, La Tambura always had the most special place in our hearts. There, seated at either end of the long table, my parents gave me a strong sense of security (and taught me to respect the ritual of mealtimes). When they held hands and smiled at each other, it seemed to me that nothing could ever feel more complete.

PAPPARDELLE WITH PHEASANT

This is the kind of hearty dish my parents would order for me as a child when we went out to eat in one of our favorite Tuscan *trattorie*. You can use other types of game, if you prefer, or the milder-tasting guinea fowl instead. Ask your butcher to joint the pheasant for you.

Serves 4 to 6
Preparation time: 20 minutes, plus
   6 hours marinating and making
   the pasta
Cooking time: 2 hours 10 minutes

1 pheasant, 3 pounds 5 ounces, cut
   into pieces
⅓ cup olive oil
8 slices of bacon or pancetta, chopped
a large pinch of freshly grated nutmeg
1 cup plus 2 tablespoons beef or game
   stock
1 recipe quantity Fresh Pasta (see
   page 162), cut into 1½-inch-wide
   long strips (pappardelle)

4 tablespoons unsalted butter
kosher salt and freshly ground
   black pepper
freshly grated Parmesan cheese,
   to serve

Marinade:
2 cups plus 2 tablespoons dry red
   wine
1 large onion, quartered
1 celery stick, quartered
5 or 6 black peppercorns
a pinch of dried thyme
2 bay leaves

Mix together the marinade ingredients in a large, nonmetallic bowl. Submerge the pheasant pieces in the marinade, then cover and leave to marinate in the refrigerator 6 hours. Drain the pheasant thoroughly, then strain the marinade through a fine strainer into a clean bowl.

Heat the oil in a large, heavy-based saucepan over medium-low heat. Add the bacon and fry gently until its fat runs out. Increase the heat to medium, add the pheasant pieces and brown them all over, then season with nutmeg, salt and pepper. Add a ladleful of the stock and simmer gently, covered, 2 hours, or until the meat is very tender. Throughout the cooking time, add the reserved marinade and stock alternately to keep the meat moist.

Just before the pheasant is cooked, bring a large saucepan of salted water to a boil. Remove the pheasant from the sauce and either leave the flesh on the bones or remove the flesh in large pieces. Cover the pheasant with foil to keep it warm and leave to one side.

Add the pasta to the boiling water and stir, then cook 3 minutes, or until al dente. Drain the pasta and return it to the saucepan. Pour the sauce over the pasta and toss together thoroughly. Add the butter and toss again. Spoon the pheasant pieces, or pieces of flesh, over the sauce-covered pasta and serve sprinkled with Parmesan.

ROASTED LANGOUSTINES

My mother loved seafood more than anything, and her insistence on keeping all dishes that use it absolutely simple is a rule to which I have always adhered. The all-important flavor of the fresh fish must shine through——that was what she always told me! I like to serve langoustines with chunky french fries and a crisp green salad dressed with a little olive oil, salt and lemon juice.

Serves 4
Preparation time: 15 minutes,
  plus 30 minutes marinating
Cooking time: 10 minutes

8 large, raw langoustines
  or jumbo shrimp
⅓ cup olive oil

2 garlic cloves, finely chopped
3 tablespoons chopped parsley leaves
juice of 1 lemon
kosher salt and freshly ground
  black pepper
wedges of lemon, to serve

Rinse the langoustines thoroughly, then cut each one open on the underside using a pair of sharp scissors and carefully remove and discard the black intestinal tract.

Put the langoustines in a shallow, nonmetallic dish. Mix together all the remaining ingredients, except the lemon wedges, in a measuring jug and pour the mixture over the langoustines. Cover and leave to marinate in the refrigerator 30 minutes.

Heat the oven to 350°F. Lay the langoustines in a shallow roasting pan and roast 10 minutes, basting frequently with the marinade and turning them occasionally, until they are cooked through. Alternatively, cook on the grill rack over a hot barbecue. Serve hot or cold with wedges of lemon.

LIGURIAN SEAFOOD SALAD

This is the sort of appetizer my parents always loved to order and one they would have undoubtedly enjoyed eating together in the early days of their courtship. Use whatever seafood is in season, as long as it's super fresh: razor clams, sea scallops, crab or small chunks of monkfish tail are all delicious additions. This dish only needs some crusty Italian bread to soak up the delicious juices and dressing.

Serves 4
Preparation time: 30 minutes,
  plus cooling
Cooking time: 25 to 30 minutes

2½ pounds mussels
2½ pounds baby clams
7 ounces dressed and prepared squid,
  cut into neat strips and rings
6 ounces small raw, shell-on shrimp

4 large raw, shell-on shrimp
juice of ½ lemon
⅓ cup extra virgin olive oil
3 tablespoons chopped parsley leaves
kosher salt and freshly ground
  black pepper
crusty bread and lemon slices,
  to serve

Scrub the mussels and clams thoroughly with a stiff brush under cold running water to remove all traces of grit, then remove any barnacles or other debris attached to the shells and pull off and discard the "beard" from the mussels. Rinse the shellfish again and discard any with broken shells or that do not close as soon as they are tapped.

Bring a saucepan of salted water to a boil. Add the squid, reduce the heat and simmer 25 to 30 minutes until tender. Drain and leave to cool. Meanwhile, put the mussels and clams and a splash of water in a large saucepan over medium heat. Cover with a tight-fitting lid and steam 8 minutes, shaking the pan occasionally, or until the shells open. Discard any that remain closed. Drain and leave the mussels and clams to cool.

Put the small shrimp in a saucepan and cover with cold water. Bring to a boil and cook 1 minute, or until they turn pink, then drain and leave to cool before peeling. Bring a separate saucepan of water to a boil, add the large shrimp and cook 2 to 3 minutes until they turn pink, then drain, shell, devein and leave to cool.

Remove the mussels and clams from their shells, then put them in a salad bowl with the shelled shrimp and squid and mix together. Add the lemon juice, oil and parsley to the seafood, season with pepper and mix well. Just before serving, season with salt and add the large shrimp. Serve with crusty bread and lemon slices.

MACKEREL WITH WHITE WINE & TOMATOES

The humble mackerel is a sadly underrated fish, but it does need to be as fresh as possible for it to really show off how wonderful it can be. Any oily or white fish works very well cooked in this way—and it was one of my parents' favorite ways of enjoying fresh fish. Making this always reminds me of them, and, like my mother before me, I serve this with garlicky pan-fried zucchini and boiled potatoes dressed with good olive oil.

Serves 6
Preparation time: 45 minutes
Cooking time: 20 to 25 minutes

6 tablespoons olive oil, plus extra
  for greasing
8 ripe tomatoes
6 large or 12 small mackerel, dressed,
  heads removed and boned
4 garlic cloves, sliced
1 handful of black olives, pitted
2 tablespoons salted capers, rinsed
  and drained
pared peel of 1 unwaxed lemon,
  chopped
7 ounces dry white wine
1 heaped teaspoon dried oregano
kosher salt and freshly ground
  black pepper
pan-fried zucchini and boiled potatoes
  dressed in olive oil, to serve

Heat the oven to 375°F. Grease a baking dish with a little oil. Cut a cross in the bottom of each tomato, using a sharp knife, then put them in a heatproof bowl and cover with boiling water. Leave to stand 2 to 3 minutes, then drain. Peel off and discard the skins, then seed and roughly chop the flesh. Leave to one side.

Rinse the mackerel and pat dry with paper towels. Lightly oil the fish inside and out with 2 tablespoons of the oil, then put half the slices of garlic, olives, capers and slivers of lemon peel inside each fish. Season with salt and pepper inside and out.

Put the mackerel in the greased dish side by side and head to tail. Sprinkle with 2 more tablespoons of the oil and the remaining garlic, olives, capers and lemon peel. Pour half the wine over, then cover with the tomatoes and sprinkle with the oregano.

Bake 15 minutes, then remove the dish from the oven and add the remaining wine. Bake 5 to 10 minutes longer until the fish is cooked through. Drizzle the fish with the remaining oil and serve with pan-fried zucchini and boiled potatoes dressed in oil.

FRESH PASTA

Remember not all eggs or batches of flour are exactly the same, so you might need to adjust the recipe quantities slightly. Other factors, such as the weather, humidity and temperature, will affect the way the pasta turns out, too. Everyone who makes pasta will make it slightly differently and each time it's made it will be a bit different to the last. You can use all Italian "00" flour, if you don't want to use half semolina flour.

Serves 4 to 6
Preparation time: 20 minutes, plus
   at least 20 minutes resting

1⅓ cups Italian "00" flour, plus extra
   for dusting

1⅓ cups semolina flour (*semola di grano duro*)
   (or use a total of scant 3 cups Italian "00" flour)
4 extra-large eggs, beaten

Mix together both types of flour on a work surface and form into a pile. Plunge your fist into the middle to make a hollow, then pour the beaten eggs into the hollow.

Using your hands and a dough scraper to avoid too much mess, draw the flour and eggs together with sweeping movements at first, then begin to knead together. Knead for about 10 minutes, or until the mixture forms a very smooth, pliable ball of dough—the dough should suddenly feel cooler and become springy. Don't overknead or it will lose its elasticity and become brittle.

Cover the dough with a clean dish towel or wrap in plastic wrap and leave to rest at least 20 minutes to relax the gluten and to make the dough more manageable.

ROLLING OUT BY HAND
Divide the dough into four pieces and wrap three of the pieces in plastic wrap. Roll out one piece of the dough as thinly as possible (about ¼ inch thick) with a strong, long rolling pin. Continue to roll until the dough is very elastic, smooth and shiny. When it is ready, the sheet of dough will feel exactly like a brand-new, slightly damp chamois leather. Leave the sheet of pasta to dry on a floured work surface about 10 minutes.

Repeat with the remaining dough. Do not let the rolled-out pasta sheets become too dry
or they will be difficult to cut. You can cover them with slightly damp, clean dish towels,
if necessary. Using a sharp knife, cut the pasta into strips or the desired shape as soon
as it is just dry enough to roll up without sticking to itself. Once cut, use immediately.

USING A PASTA MACHINE
If you are using a hand-cranked pasta machine, make the dough and leave it to rest at least
20 minutes as before. When the dough has rested, unwrap it and cut off a piece about the
size of a small fist, then re-wrap the remaining dough.

Flatten out the piece of dough with your hands, then feed it through the widest setting of
your pasta machine. Fold the pasta in half widthwise and feed it through the rollers again.
Do this twice more, or until you hear the pasta "snap" as the rollers force the tiny air pockets
to burst and make a sound. When this happens, turn the machine down to the next setting
and feed the dough through the machine twice more.

Continue to feed the dough through the rollers, reducing the setting by one notch after every
second time, until the last or penultimate setting on the machine, depending on how fine
you want the pasta to be. If the pasta becomes too long to manage easily, cut it in half
widthwise. Leave the sheet of pasta to dry on a floured work surface about 10 minutes.

Repeat with the remaining dough. Do not let the rolled-out pasta sheets become too dry
or they will be difficult to cut. You can cover them with slightly damp, clean dish towels
if necessary. Using a sharp knife, cut the pasta into strips or the desired shape as soon
as it is just dry enough to roll up without sticking to itself. Once cut, use immediately.

Pictured from left my cousins Caroline and Tim; me;
my brother Howard (Din); Rosanna; Andreina with
her son Antonio; Molly; and Beppino.

14. *Beppino,*
THE MASTER OF RISOTTO

Beppino was one of the Italian refugees left stranded in the aftermath of the war, after the fall of the Fascist regime. He had somehow ended up living in the ruins of what became our Tuscan home, La Tambura. The house is on the coast of La Versilia, between the towns of Forte dei Marmi and Marina di Massa, with the Carrara mountains standing proud behind it. When the weather is clear, the mountains almost seem like they are in the garden and, from the beach at the right time of day, if you get the angle spot-on, they can look as though they are rising majestically out of the sea itself.

When my mother and father first arrived at La Tambura in 1953 (with my older brothers, half-brother and a menagerie of friends and relatives in tow), Beppino alone, among all the refugees found eking out an existence in the ruins of the house and gardens, was allowed to stay on. I shall never really know what it was that made my father decide he could stay, but I do know the influence he had on all of our lives, but most especially mine, remains as true today as it was then.

Beppino was born in the Veneto. His home was in the countryside near Vicenza, where his mother bred geese. Before being called up to fight for his country, he had been a very young chef in charge of risotto at Savini, a lovely old-fashioned restaurant that still exists in the Galleria, in Milan. Risotto is a shared regional dish of the Veneto, Piedmont and Lombardy, and Beppino taught me how to make it when I was just a little girl with grazed knees and pockets full of treasures like fresh peas in the pod or a much-gnawed Parmesan rind. He taught me so many things: how to make wine, bread and olive oil; grow vegetables; care for rabbits and chickens; respect the environment; and avoid any

> He taught me so many things: how to make wine, bread and olive oil; grow vegetables; care for rabbits and chickens...

"*porcherie,*" which is what he called any food that had been messed about with and not homemade and traceable in origin. He was my inspiration, and still is in so many ways, especially when I make a risotto in his time-honored way.

On July 14, 1957, Beppino opened the battered green gates of La Tambura so my father could drive through, at the end of one of our many epic journeys. (My father was constantly moving his entire entourage from country to country, being peripatetic by nature. It was tiresome being packed for long hours in the car, but it did allow my mother to plan what she called "Le Tour Gastronomique.") Seconds later, I was placed, just ten days old, in Beppino's arms. It was the start of a relationship that was to last for many years and, in a way, to launch my career in food.

I have never known anyone who could work as hard as Beppino, or do so many brilliantly useful things in one day. He not only rebuilt the house single-handedly, which had suffered enormously from bombing during the war, but also established our luscious vegetable garden; restored the fruit trees and vines; and created a chicken coop, rabbit hutches and a pigsty. The only time I ever witnessed Beppino taking a break from his work was the day he broke his foot and was taken off to the hospital to be plastered, roaring angrily all the way. I found him hours later in his hut, hacking off the plaster with an axe and binding the poor, broken foot in wet paper instead, all the while assuring me it would heal much better that way.

In between the chicken coop and the pigsty was the still, where Beppino would illegally distill grappa, his favorite tipple. I would sit for hours on the floor of this little hut, chin in hands, watching the pale, golden liquid curling its way around the spiraling glass pipe, waiting patiently with Beppino for the moment when it would flow out the other end, ready to taste. The logic of putting the still in that location was that the telltale smell of the alcohol would be masked by the all-pervasive pong of the chickens and pigs should any person of authority pay a visit. I would worry endlessly about the still being found, but Beppino would just swig another mouthful of the fiery liquid and laugh at my concerns.

I followed Beppino around from morning to night, helping him work in the vegetable patch; clipping the vines; clearing out the animals' bedding for manure; sweeping the pathways clear of pine needles; cutting wood; and repairing anything anywhere that needed mending. I would especially love digging over the ground in the chicken coop and watching our hens gobble up the fat earthworms that wriggled up to the light as the earth was turned. Together, we grew zucchini, green beans, salad leaves, tomatoes and cabbages. I would always know when winter had truly arrived because that was when

Andreina and Beppino with me at
La Tambura.

La Tambura.

there was nothing left in the vegetable garden, except the tall, frosted leaves of the cavolo nero, immobile and dark in the freezing air.

Beppino showed me how to wring a chicken's or rabbit's neck, a quick twist against a bent knee and it was all over, the animal ready to be prepared for the pot. Still warm, we would hang the animal upside down on the vine wires, Beppino choosing carefully a spot between two vines that needed extra fertilization. Then he would fetch his big, flat spade and dig a deep hole directly under the rabbit

> **... Beppino would decree it was a good day for fishing. So, at sunset, we would ride our bicycles down to the beach...**

or chicken. Under his guidance, I would then pluck the bird or skin and gut the animal, taking care that everything that was not meat would fall directly into the pit we had dug, which we would then cover over carefully when finished. The chicken, or rabbit, would then be washed repeatedly in well water, one of us pumping while the other did the washing, and then finally carried proudly into the kitchen. It was not long before I could do all of this myself, and always relished the opportunity.

At certain times of the year, by watching the sky and feeling the air in his own inimitable way, Beppino would decree it was a good day for fishing. So, at sunset, we would ride our bicycles down to the beach and row out on a *pattino*, a small, flat kind of very light catamaran without sails, the nets piled in a huge coiled heap on the platform between the two prows. I always wanted to be the person responsible for dropping the first flagged buoy, which indicated one end of the net, into the water. Then, slowly and carefully, we would let the net fall into the sea as we rowed expertly around in a horseshoe shape, the *pattino* seriously overloaded with passengers, finally dropping the second buoy at the other end. Job done, and the sky almost dark, we would return home—sandy, salty and very wet—on our rickety old bicycles, hopefully just in time for dinner.

The next morning at dawn, Beppino would gently shake me awake. Still salty and sandy from the night before, I would pedal behind him (with anybody else who could be bothered to get up so early), back down to the beach. There we would push the *pattino* into the sea and row out again, coiling the wet nets from the water onto the platform, then heading back toward the shore once we had finished hauling. The sun would just be rising, bathing the Carrara mountains, which form the eternal magical backdrop to this strip of coast. The dawn light was vibrant and the palest violet, covering the surface of the sea with a mother-of-pearl sheen and making the marble on the mountains glow intensely as though they were on fire.

The only other people ever on the beach at this magical time would be the nuns from the local convent, splashing noisily around in the waves in their wimples and ample, black knitted bathing costumes. Beppino and the other men would turn their eyes away in respect, crossing themselves as they did so, but the children of the party would gape, open-mouthed, at the frolicking sisters.

Back on the beach, we would all line up on the *bagnasciuga*, the wave-lapped sandy shoreline, studded with marble pebbles, each of us with our own bucket. We were instructed firmly to remove only the type of fish assigned specifically to us from the nets. For some reason, I always got to do the squid, and I still have scars all over my hands from where they buried their sharp black beaks into my soft, girlie fingers! Hand over hand, crouched low, with our bottoms just dipping in the water, we would pass the nets from one to another, removing the fish with great care so as not to tear the net or damage our precious haul, and safely drop the catch into the buckets, half filled with fresh, cool seawater to keep it fresh.

The biggest hazard was always the sand weever, or *tracina*. This fish is tasty enough when added to a fish soup, but its defense mechanism entails it burying itself just under the sand at low tide, leaving its nasty spines poking up through the sand. It then spends its time just waiting for a tender foot to press down on the spines before releasing its poison into the flesh, and from there into the bloodstream. It is an excruciatingly painful thing to happen, and many a happy day on the beach has ended for me in the agony of a sand weever accident. The immediate cure is a bucket of hot water in which to soak the foot and draw out the poison, followed by a dousing in nausea-inducing ammonia, liberally poured over the tiny, innocuous-looking puncture wounds. All this administered by the handsome beach attendant—*il bagnino*—with great drama, and plenty of people watching and adding their opinion. There were always lots of sand weevers in our nets and I always felt really sorry for whoever had the job of disentangling them, as they inevitably got spiked. Sometimes, one of my squid would have a sand weever hanging half in and half out of its beak. I would prise it out carefully, taking care not to touch the dead fish, even though everybody told me it could no longer hurt me.

Once the nets were emptied of all the fish, they needed washing and cleaning in the sea before being carefully coiled up again, ready for the next time. The contents of our buckets would then be checked over, and Beppino would start the job

... warm fresh bread and bowls of caffè latte awaited us... Preparation of the great fish lunch would then begin.

of deciding how we would cook our catch. Was there enough for a *fritto misto*? A pasta sauce? A risotto? *Zuppa*? Or crostini topping? Before the sun became too hot and our catch lost its freshness, we would pedal home again, balancing our buckets precariously on the handlebars and avoiding any bumps, to prevent seawater or the fish slopping out onto the road.

Back in the kitchen, warm fresh bread and bowls of caffè latte awaited us, and all the adults would wave around tiny cups of espresso laced with grappa to emphasize and punctuate their words as they continued the discussion as to what delicious dishes we were going to turn our fresh bounty into. Preparation of the great fish lunch would then begin. There would be herbs and vegetables to find in the garden, potatoes to peel and the table to be set. I would watch Beppino's knife flying through onions on the cutting board, and try hard to match his speed. There were always jobs for me to do, and very little praise handed out, which made any compliments especially precious. Mainly, he would say things like: "Ha! You'd make a restaurant bankrupt in a day, wasting food like you do!" if I removed too much flesh off a potato as I peeled it, or sliced a lemon too thickly.

Finally, at lunchtime, sitting in my place at the table, I would feel such a sense of pride and anticipation swell within me as the food was brought in, and I would bask happily in everyone's obvious enjoyment and pleasure. Yet, somehow I knew that all the while it would be Beppino who was having the best meal, under a tree in the garden, enjoying his especially chosen morsels—things that nobody else, except possibly me, would really appreciate —and blissfully alone.

BAKED ZUCCHINI WITH TOMATOES & MOZZARELLA

This recipe really celebrates for me the memory of the fragrant tomatoes and zucchini that would grow in our vegetable garden at La Tambura, so lovingly tended by Beppino. This is a lighter version of the classic Italian dish, *Parmigiana di melanzane,* which uses eggplants.

Serves 4
Preparation time: 30 minutes,
   plus 1 hour standing
Cooking time: 1 hour 10 minutes

4 or 5 medium to large zucchini,
   trimmed and sliced diagonally
2 tablespoons all-purpose flour
1 cup plus 2 tablespoons sunflower
   oil
7 ounces mozzarella cheese, drained
   and finely chopped

Tomato sauce:
8 ripe tomatoes
2 tablespoons olive oil
½ onion, chopped
1 handful of basil leaves, torn into
   shreds
a large pinch of dried oregano
kosher salt and freshly ground
   black pepper

Put the zucchini in a large colander and sprinkle with salt, then leave to stand 1 hour.

Meanwhile, cut a cross in the bottom of each tomato, using a sharp knife, then put them in a heatproof bowl and cover with boiling water. Leave to stand 2 to 3 minutes, then drain. Peel off and discard the skins, then seed and roughly chop the flesh.

To make the tomato sauce, heat the olive oil in a skillet. Add the onion and fry until very soft, then stir in the tomatoes, basil and oregano and season with salt and pepper. Cover and simmer 30 minutes, or until thick. Press the sauce through a strainer into a bowl.

While the sauce is simmering, rinse the zucchini well and pat dry with paper towels. Put them in a bowl and toss lightly in the flour. Heat the sunflower oil in a large skillet over medium heat until a small cube of bread dropped into the oil sizzles instantly. Working in batches, if necessary, to avoid overcrowding the pan, add the zucchini and fry until golden brown. Remove from the pan using a slotted spoon and drain well on paper towels.

Heat the oven to 350°F. Cover the bottom of a baking dish with a layer of the sauce, then add a layer of fried zucchini, then a layer of mozzarella. Repeat the layers until all the ingredients are used. Bake 30 minutes, or until heated through.

SEAFOOD RISOTTO

Serves 4 to 6
Preparation time: 40 minutes
Cooking time: about 1 hour

1 pound 2 ounces mussels
1 pound 2 ounces baby clams
2 cups dry white wine
5½ cups strong fish stock
⅔ cup extra virgin olive oil
9 ounces raw, shell-on small shrimp
9 ounces raw, shell-on langoustines
  or large shrimp
½ dry red chili, finely chopped
3 garlic cloves, finely chopped
4 tablespoons chopped parsley leaves,
  plus extra to serve
2½ cups carnaroli rice
kosher salt and freshly ground
  black pepper

Scrub the mussels and clams thoroughly with a stiff brush under cold running water to remove all traces of grit, then remove any barnacles or other debris attached to the shells and pull off and discard the "beard" from the mussels. Rinse the shellfish again and discard any with broken shells or that do not close as soon as they are tapped.

Pour one-quarter of the wine into a deep skillet and bring to a boil over medium heat. Add the clams and steam, covered, for a few minutes until the shells open, discarding any that remain closed. Remove from the heat, take the clams out of their shells and discard the shells. Leave to one side. Repeat with the mussels, leaving half in the shell. Strain the juices in the pan through a strainer into a pitcher. Meanwhile, put the fish stock in a pan and warm through.

Pour 2 to 3 tablespoons of the oil into a skillet and briefly fry the shrimp over medium heat, turning frequently and basting with some of the wine, until bright pink. Shell the shrimp, adding the shells and heads to the simmering fish stock. Leave to one side. Repeat with the langoustines, cooking them 5 minutes until they turn orange-pink. Take them out of the pan and remove the claws and tails. Open out the tails and remove the flesh, discarding the black intestinal tract that runs along the back. Leave the flesh to one side. Add the heads and shells to the hot stock and simmer 5 minutes, then strain the stock into a pan and keep hot.

Heat the remaining oil in the skillet over medium heat. Add the chili, garlic and parsley and fry 2 minutes, then add the rice. Stir until combined, then add another quarter of the wine. Cook 2 minutes, or until the alcohol evaporates, stirring. Stir in the juices from the clams and mussels and cook until the rice absorbs the liquid. Add the rest of the wine and cook, adding the stock a ladleful at a time, over medium-low heat 10 minutes, stirring continuously. Add the cooked seafood, then continue to cook, adding the stock gradually and stirring until the rice is creamy but still firm in the middle, about 10 minutes. Season with salt and pepper and serve sprinkled with extra parsley.

FRIED ZUCCHINI FLOWERS
(*FIORI DI ZUCCA*)

As Beppino always loved to show me, both the female and the male zucchini produce flowers and they are easy to distinguish. The male flower is at the end of a long stalk, which is attached to the stem of the plant, whereas the female flower is attached to the zucchini itself. Male flowers are easier to use in this recipe, as you can hold the stalk while you dip the flower in the batter, but both types taste equally delicious. In either case, check the flowers on the inside for bugs before starting, and always remove the pistil, which tastes bitter.

Serves 4
Preparation time: about 30 minutes
Cooking time: about 15 minutes

2½ cups sunflower oil
12 to 16 zucchini flowers, cleaned
  and pistils removed
kosher salt

Batter:
1 egg

2 tablespoons all-purpose flour
⅔ cup milk, or half milk and half
  water mixed together

Filling (optional):
4 to 5 tablespoons ricotta
  or ½ cup mozzarella cheese cut into
  1¼-inch cubes
6 to 8 anchovy fillets in oil, drained
  and cut into ¼-inch pieces

To make the batter, separate the egg into two bowls, then cover and chill the egg white. Beat together the egg yolk, flour and milk in a mixing bowl to make a smooth paste. In a separate bowl, whisk the egg white until stiff, then fold it into the egg yolk batter.

Heat the oil in a large, deep skillet over medium-high heat until a small cube of bread dropped into the oil sizzles instantly.

Meanwhile, if filling the flowers, tuck 1 teaspoon of the ricotta (or a piece of mozzarella) and a piece of anchovy into each courgette flower. Holding the flowers by their stalks or ends, carefully dip them into the batter to coat thoroughly. If the flowers have been stuffed, fold down the petals of each flower and use the batter to secure the filling in place.

Working in batches, if necessary, to avoid overcrowding the pan, carefully lower the batter-coated flowers into the hot oil. Fry 3 to 4 minutes, turning frequently, until crisp and golden all over. Remove from the pan using a slotted spoon and drain well on paper towels. Serve the fried flowers sprinkled with a little salt.

Above, La Tambura in spring.
Right, my brothers, Howard (Din) and
Nick at the green gates of La Tambura.

15. THE DOGS ARE BARKING AT THE MILKMAN, *Marietto*

There was something very special about the green gates of La Tambura. Once you had closed them behind you, it was as if you were shutting out the rest of the world. It made every arrival feel like a real homecoming; when you came through the gates you were welcomed into a place where nothing really bad could ever happen and where good food and serenity were the order of the day.

Conversely, stepping outside the gates always gave me a real frisson of adventure, a sense of being out in the bigger world where anything could happen. There was a smaller pair of similar gates, hidden in a corner of the grounds, but my father had them sealed closed after I had slipped through them one too many times after dark, flouting his strict curfew.

Although my nighttime escapades were fun, I was always happiest inside those green gates: helping out in the kitchen, which always seemed to be buzzing with preparations for the next group of guests; or sleeping between bouts of cooking when there was a pause, the white chairs upended on the marble table to let the terracotta floor dry.

In our corner of Tuscany in the early 1960s when I was a little girl, milk was not sold in the pyramid-shaped cartons we had in Rome (which were almost impossible to snip open or use without causing a huge mess). In the city, we had to buy them from the *latteria*, along with other dairy produce, such as the incredibly sour, thin, plain yogurt and deliciously light-tasting unsalted butter. Cheese was something available only at the *salumeria* or the *alimentari*, neither of which sold milk. It was confusing, but only to the uninitiated. Shopping was a long-winded affair in those days, much more laborious than a quick dash around the supermarket, but it meant food and cooking were held in the highest regard; and after all the effort of acquiring the ingredients, wasting anything was considered almost sinful.

> Shopping was a long-winded affair in those days, much more laborious than a quick dash around the supermarket.

One of the highlights of being at La Tambura was the daily delivery of milk, which never failed to entertain me, as it managed to turn a simple glass of milk into a real event. To start at the very beginning of the story of Marietto, our milkman at La Tambura, we have to go back to when Beppino was stranded in the ruins of the house at the end of the war. With him were a few other waifs and strays, all of them victims of the dying days of war. When my mother and father arrived, and only Beppino was allowed to stay, the rest of the group stayed close by. One of them was Marietto, who kept dairy cows on a ramshackle smallholding.

Marietto had a terrible singing voice and a penchant for drinking too much wine. He drove a rackety old Ape, piled high with the brown, dried pine needles that he had collected from people's gardens and which he used as bedding for his cows. He would arrive at our gates twice a day, morning and evening, singing so loudly he almost drowned out the sound of his engine. His arrival caused the dogs to go mad with barking. There were always three or four hanging around, mostly strays that Andreina, Beppino's wife, had found and brought home—but there was also my own dog, a beautiful and utterly daft Irish Setter called Chuff. Hearing the racket, I would take down the battered old milk pan from the smooth marble kitchen windowsill and race to the gate to greet him.

Marietto's evening delivery was always more perilous than the morning one, as he would be offered a *quartino* (a quarter of a liter of wine) at each household he visited on his way to ours, so by the time he got to us he was well and truly drunk. Then he would lurch out of the cab of his Ape and grab one of the milk churns from the back, which he unscrewed before trying to aim a stream of milk into my pan. A lot of the precious milk would splash onto the ground, however deftly I moved the pan around, trying to follow his wavering movements to catch it. Once full, I would tiptoe back to the kitchen with it like a tightrope walker, trying hard not to spill too much. The milk would then be boiled and left to stand and cool.

Whenever I taste boiled milk, the memory of that sweet and creamy unpasteurized milk of Marietto's comes flooding back. And even now, after half a century, whenever I arrive in Italy I feel an almost overpowering need to reengage with this country I love so passionately—through its food. The feeling is not tied to a specific dish; it is the ingredients themselves that comfort me. I am reassured beyond all imagination I am home again.

Above, from left my mom, Caroline, Tim, me, Howard (Din), Molly and Aunt Leonora.

PORK BRAISED IN MILK

Many versions of this dish exist all over Italy; some include cloves or other spices, but this is the way Beppino would make it. The Dutch oven you use should be of a size and shape that will comfortably take the meat and all the milk, allowing the meat to remain mostly submerged in the liquid while it cooks. It requires long, slow cooking to render the meat truly tender until it almost starts to fall apart.

Serves 4 to 6
Preparation time: 20 minutes
Cooking time: about 2½ hours

¼ cup sunflower oil
3 pounds pork loin, skin removed
  and trimmed of fat
3 tablespoons cooking brandy
4 large garlic cloves, thinly sliced
1 handful of sage leaves

5½ cups milk, plus extra as needed
thinly pared peel of 2 unwaxed
  lemons
juice of 1 lemon
kosher salt and freshly ground
  black pepper
apple compote and mashed potatoes,
  to serve

Heat the oven to 400°F. Heat the oil in a large Dutch oven over medium heat. Add the pork loin and sear until brown all over, then add the brandy and leave it to bubble a few minutes until the alcohol evaporates. Remove the pot from the heat, then take out the pork and drain the fat from the pot.

Return the pork to the pot and add the garlic and sage, then season with salt and pepper and pour in the milk to cover the meat. Return the dish to the heat and bring to a boil, then remove the pot from the heat and add the lemon peel and juice.

Leave the milk to curdle slightly, then cover the pot, transfer it to the oven and bake 20 minutes. Reduce the temperature to 300°F and bake 1½ hours longer, adding more milk as necessary and basting and turning the pork every 20 to 30 minutes, or until tender.

Leave the pork to rest in the pot 5 minutes, then carve the meat and spoon the milky juices from the dish over the top. Serve with apple compote and mashed potatoes.

MILK & RICE SOUP

As little children we were given this silky, savory rice soup, especially at times when the Tuscan damp seeped into our bones and it was almost impossible to get warm. A handful of crumbled chestnuts would sometimes be added, too.

Serves 4
Preparation time: 5 minutes
Cooking time: about 20 minutes

4¼ cups milk
1 cup risotto rice

3 tablespoons unsalted butter
½ teaspoon kosher salt
¼ cup freshly grated Parmesan
  cheese

Put the milk in a saucepan and bring to a boil. Immediately add the rice, half the butter and the salt. Reduce the heat to low and simmer very gently 20 minutes, stirring frequently, until the rice is creamy and tender. Remove the pan from the heat and stir in the remaining butter and the cheese, then serve.

CAULIFLOWER COOKED IN MILK

Serves 4
Preparation time: about 20 minutes
Cooking time: about 20 minutes

1 large cauliflower, trimmed
1 tablespoon pine nuts
3 tablespoons unsalted butter
scant ¼ teaspoon freshly grated
  nutmeg

1 cup milk
⅓ cup freshly grated Parmesan cheese
kosher salt and freshly ground
  black pepper

Bring a large saucepan of salted water to a boil. Add the cauliflower, bring back to a boil and cook for 3 minutes, then drain and leave to cool.

Meanwhile, heat the broiler to medium. Put the pine nuts on a cookie sheet and broil until lightly toasted, checking frequently to make sure they don't burn. Leave to one side.

Break the cauliflower into small florets. Melt the butter in a large skillet over medium heat. Add the florets, season with salt, pepper and the nutmeg, then stir well to coat them in the butter. Pour in the milk, then reduce the heat to low and simmer until the cauliflower is very soft, about 10 minutes. Sprinkle with the Parmesan and pine nuts and serve hot.

SPINACH & BREAD GNOCCHI

This is one of Beppino's wife Andreina's greatest dishes, and it is wonderfully fun to make. The milk is an essential part of the dish, even though it is only used to soak the stale bread.

Serves 4 to 6
Preparation time: 45 minutes
Cooking time: about 15 minutes

5 ounces stale white bread
scant 2 cups milk
3 pounds 5 ounces fresh spinach, washed
1 egg and 2 egg yolks, beaten

2 tablespoons light cream (or use the milk from the soaked bread)
1½ cups freshly grated Parmesan cheese
¼ teaspoon freshly grated nutmeg
about ⅓ cup all-purpose flour
scant ½ cup unsalted butter
kosher salt and freshly ground black pepper

Put the bread in a large bowl, pour the milk over to cover and leave to soak until soft. Squeeze the bread as dry as possible with your hands and leave to one side. At the same time, steam the spinach in a large saucepan until tender, then drain and leave to cool. Squeeze out as much water as possible, then chop the spinach finely or blitz it in a food processor. Put the spinach in a large bowl and stir in the egg and egg yolks, then the cream. Add the bread and half the cheese and season with the nutmeg and salt and pepper, then combine together.

Bring a small saucepan of salted water to a boil. To test if the mixture is the correct consistency, wet the inside of a small glass with water, then lightly dust with flour, but do not overflour or the gnocchi will be rubbery. Drop a tablespoon of the mixture into the glass and shake the glass, tilting it to shape the mixture into gnocchi. Repeat with another tablespoon of the mixture. Drop the gnocchi into the boiling water—they should float to the surface in about 2 minutes, hold their shape and taste flavorsome. If not, adjust the remaining mixture by adding more egg or a little flour, or both, and extra salt and pepper, if needed.

When the correct texture is achieved, continue shaping the remaining mixture in the glass, reflouring it as necessary, and lay the gnocchi out on a floured cookie sheet, spacing them well apart. Chill until required.

Heat the oven to its lowest setting. Bring a large saucepan of salted water to a boil. Working in small batches, slip the gnocchi into the pan and cook about 2 minutes until they float to the surface. Scoop out with a slotted spoon and keep warm in the oven. Continue until all the gnocchi are cooked. Meanwhile, melt the butter in a small saucepan. Pour it over the gnocchi, sprinkle with the remaining Parmesan and serve.

CARAMEL MILK PUDDING

Known in Italian as *latte alle Portuguese*, this is one of those desserts that never fails to bring back many happy memories from my childhood. It was a wonderful way of using our milkman, Marietto's, milk to create something so simple and yet so perfectly delicious. My mother loved to make this, and would curse when it split as she turned it out, as it inevitably did!

Serves 4
Preparation time: 45 minutes,
   plus cooling and at least
   2 hours chilling
Cooking time: 1 hour 15 minutes

4½ cups milk
1 unwaxed lemon, peel pared off
   in a single spiral and white pith
   removed

⅓ cup granulated sugar
6 eggs
¼ cup plus 2 tablespoons superfine
   sugar

Put the milk and the lemon peel in a saucepan and bring to a boil, then remove the pan from the heat and leave the milk to cool completely. Discard the lemon peel.

Meanwhile, make the caramel. Put the granulated sugar in a 6½-cup fluted metal ring mold and add 2 tablespoons water. Put the mold over medium heat and, holding it with tongs and an oven mitt, rotate the mold, tilting it from side to side to make sure the sugar coats the sides as it melts and turns a hazelnut brown color. This will take 10 to 15 minutes. Remove the mold from the heat and leave to cool completely. (Alternatively, make the caramel in a small, heavy-based saucepan, then pour it into the ring mold, tilting it to coat the sides and continue as below.)

Heat the oven to 325°F. Whisk the eggs in a large bowl until thick and pale, then gradually whisk in the superfine sugar and cool milk. Carefully pour the mixture into the mold containing the caramel, then put the mold in a roasting pan. Pour enough boiling water into the pan to come two-thirds up the sides of the mold.

Bake 1 hour, topping up the water as necessary, until a skewer inserted into the middle comes out clean. Leave to cool completely, then chill at least 2 hours before serving.

Me enjoying the sun in my first bikini!

16. SUMMER NIGHTS AT THE CINEMA
Romanina

In those long hot summers at La Tambura, when I was about ten years old, it was our custom to retire to the living room after dinner to play liar dice or charades, or just to chat. There were always so many people staying at the house it buzzed; and there was invariably somebody with whom to talk or to persuade to join in the entertainment. Sometimes, a game of sardines in the dense vegetation and dark shadows of the garden would be instigated by one of my brothers; or we would grab the bikes on ferociously hot nights and pedal very slowly down to the beach to skinny dip. We swam in the almost bath-temperature water, often shining with phosphorescence, under a shower of bright shooting stars, the mountains behind us decorated with apricot-colored strings of streetlights, far up in the tiny, distant villages.

On other nights, I would long to join my friend Rossana and her brother at the cinema. It was not actually a cinema in the true sense of the word; the movies were shown in the church of a boys-only *colonia* across our street and halfway down a little lane that led to the beach. It was called La Romanina and, like *colonie* everywhere in Italy, it existed to give children a summer vacation their parents otherwise might not be able to afford. These institutions operated a bit like summer camps, and used to exist all over Italy, run either by religious orders or by large corporations, like Fiat or Olivetti, to offer the factory workers' children the chance of a proper vacation. In 1822, the Hospital of Lucca launched the first organized seaside vacation for the street children of Viareggio. The idea caught

> ... or we would grab the bikes on ferociously hot nights and pedal very slowly down to the beach to skinny dip.

on and by the middle of the 1800s there were about fifty such *colonie* in Tuscany and Emilia Romagna, and they became especially popular during the Fascist regime. These days, although they still exist, the actual term "*colonia*" is rarely used, as it still retains the link, in some peoples' minds at least, with Mussolini.

The Colonia Romanina was run by fairly modern-thinking monks. On certain nights of the week, epic movies of a religious nature, such as Liliana Cavani's *Life of St. Francis of Assisi*, were shown—although quite often the biblical connection was more tenuous, as it was in *Ben Hur*, *Anthony and Cleopatra*, or the marvelously titled spaghetti western, *Between God, the Devil and a Winchester*. The movies, projected against the stucco wall of the little church within the Romanina, were for the entertainment of the boys vacationing at the camp, not for the general public. Our challenge was to get inside to watch the movie without getting caught by one of the brothers.

Rossana is my oldest friend, and Beppino's daughter. Her mother, Andreina, was the undisputed leader of our little gang, which was made up of Rossana and her brother Antonio, several of their cousins and me. On cinema nights, Andreina used to love the whole clandestine aspect of our outing, and seemed to want to go almost more than we did.

Andreina was a second mother to me. As our housekeeper, she ran the house with an iron rod, and she was one of those people who never seem to walk anywhere if they can run instead. As a child, I took her incredible, fizzing energy, and ability to do so many things at once in the course of her day, completely for granted. (Only now I can understand and sympathize with how tired she must have got, and how justified were her complaints of an aching back and pounding head.) But on those nights when she had made up her mind she would be going to the Romanina to watch a movie after dinner, nothing would stop her: Andreina became like a whirlwind and completed her myriad tasks even more quickly than usual.

Although Andreina took care of a hundred different household jobs, it was as a cook she was most inspirational. Beppino, as a former restaurant chef, had taught her how to make many dishes over the years, although she always got him to make those ones he was especially good at, thereby revealing a tiny, rare chink in the armor she wore as quintessential superwoman. I spent my childhood running in and out of Beppino and Andreina's house, which was situated on the other side of the huge vegetable garden.

I always offered to help her whenever she needed it, learning all kinds of ways of carrying out household tasks, every one of them like her: perfect and very quick. There is a particular way of making a bed I learned from her

Me fishing near La Tambura.

where you fold a section of the bedspread back over itself before adding the pillows, then quickly flip it back into place with one swift, neat and specific movement. My rapid shirt-ironing technique, where I always do the sleeves first, is one she taught me; and even the way I mop a floor by wrapping a cloth around the mop head and rinsing it after exactly 15 strokes is hers. I never realized any of these methods were unusual until other people picked me up on them.

... the figs would be washed and laid on platters, surrounded by mounds of pink, paper-thin slices of prosciutto.

Despite her insistence Beppino should often be the one to cook, Andreina made delicious things to eat, and I can still taste them now if I think back. Her pizza—especially the one with the caramelized white onions (see page 193)—is, without question, one of the loveliest things I have ever tasted, even if sometimes she would cheat by leaping on her bicycle and racing off to the nearest pizzeria to buy raw dough because she had run out of time to let hers rise. I do not think anybody has ever made a simple plate of Tomato, Basil & Eggplant Spaghettini (see page 194) taste as sensational; but her own favorite was her Chickpea Flour Farinata (see page 196), a flat, baked "pancake," which she made whenever she craved it.

Andreina's mother, Giulia, lived up the road; and she, as far as I was concerned, was the queen of summer afternoon cakes. Her repertoire consisted of only two types; but her moist, eggy, boozy *Torta di Riso* (Rice Cake, see page 197) is still the best teatime treat I have ever tasted. Whenever figs were on the menu, Rossana and I would have baskets thrust into our arms and Andreina would almost chase us out of the gate on our bicycles to go and pick the ripe green and black fruit from Giulia's garden. The trees were treacherous to climb, as the trunk of a fig is so smooth and slippery, but once up in the branches, lying flat with our legs dangling—eating far more figs than were good for us and not picking nearly quickly enough—we would lose ourselves in the green canopy of leaves and only Giulia shouting up that we would be late would get us to come down again. Then we would wobble home, our baskets almost too heavy to balance on the handlebars, where the figs would be washed and laid on platters, surrounded by mounds of pink, paper-thin slices of prosciutto. As we hurried to prepare the food, Andreina would scold us for delaying things, especially if it was on an evening she had decided she wanted to go to Romanina.

If I wanted to go to the cinema, I first had to get permission from my dad. He would make me promise that I would be home by 10.30 p.m., without fail. Once that was agreed, we all had to plaster ourselves in mosquito repellent from head to foot while the dishwashing and clearing the table was done at record speed. Inevitably, we would turn up at the gate of the *colonia* after the movie had begun, but this made it easier to creep in unnoticed.

We would squeeze through the gate and slip quietly around the back of a hedge, where we would perch to watch the movie, which flickered against the stucco, the actors' faces distorted by the rough-textured surface of the church wall. Behind the soundtrack, which bounced off the walls of all the surrounding buildings, we could hear the sound of the waves crashing on the beach in the distance. It was bliss! And the enjoyment of the actual movie was only heightened by the fear of discovery.

There was only one problem: I was often late back. I was always so engrossed in the movie—and the other thrilling drama in my own head where I would play out the possibility of our being caught—that I never thought to check the time. Only once we had sneaked out of the gate under cover of the closing titles would I discover that I had broken my father's curfew, and a cold terror would descend on my high spirits. With my heart pounding, I would fly down the lane in my flip-flops to get to the corner of the street as fast as I could, where I would see him standing on the pavement outside the gates to La Tambura, looking at his watch. A quick *buonanotte* to Andreina and the rest of the gang, who would slip off to their own house before my father's temper included them, and I would go and face him, ready for the ticking off and prepared for my punishment that usually

> ... we would turn up at the gate of the *colonia* after the movie had begun, but this made it easier to creep in unnoticed.

included not being allowed to go the movies again for a while. For a time, I would behave and stay home, but the lure of the Colonia Romanina always proved too much, and soon I would be working on new ways to get there.

PIZZA WITH CARAMELIZED WHITE ONIONS

Andreina's pizza, with its thick layer of deliciously sweet white onions, was very special indeed. I also like to top it with crumbled Gorgonzola.

Serves 4
Preparation time: 30 minutes, plus 30 minutes fermenting and 1 hour rising
Cooking time: 50 minutes

4 large white onions, sliced
¼ cup extra virgin olive oil
2 tablespoons semolina
kosher salt and freshly ground black pepper

thyme sprigs, to serve

Dough:
1 ounce fresh yeast or 1 envelope (¼-oz.) active dry yeast
3 cups white bread flour, plus extra for dusting
½ teaspoon sugar
1 teaspoon kosher salt
2 tablespoons extra virgin olive oil

Put the onions in a bowl, cover with cold water and leave to soak while you make the dough.

Mix together the yeast and 7 ounces warm water in a small bowl, then stir in 2 tablespoons of the flour and the sugar. Leave to stand in a warm place 30 minutes, or until the mixture begins to fizz or bubble. Put the remaining flour on a work surface and make a well in the middle. Pour the yeast mixture, salt and oil into the well in the flour and mix together, adding more warm water, if necessary, until it forms a soft but not sticky dough. Knead 10 minutes until smooth and elastic, then transfer to a large floured bowl. Cover with plastic wrap and leave to rise in a warm place about 1 hour, or until double in size.

While the dough is rising, drain the onions and pat dry in a dish towel. Heat 2 tablespoons of the oil in a large skillet. Add the onions and cook 40 minutes over very low heat, stirring frequently, until pale golden. Season with salt and pepper, then leave to one side.

Heat the oven to 400°F. Grease a large cookie sheet with 1 tablespoon of the oil, then sprinkle with the semolina. Turn the tray upside down and tap to remove any excess. When the dough has risen, knock it back on a floured work surface. Using wet hands, press the dough out into a thin circle on the prepared cookie sheet. Scatter the onions over the top and drizzle with the remaining oil. Bake 10 minutes, or until the crust is crisp. Serve hot, sprinkled with a few sprigs of thyme.

TOMATO, BASIL & EGGPLANT SPAGHETTINI

Of the many amazing pasta sauces that Beppino and Andreina would prepare for us at La Tambura, this is one of the most memorable and delicious. It is a really treasured recipe, and one that I have made many times over the years.

Serves 4
Preparation time: 25 minutes, plus 1 hour standing
Cooking time: 45 minutes

1 large eggplant, cubed
2¼ pounds ripe tomatoes, halved
1 large celery stick, quartered
1 large carrot, quartered
1 large onion, quartered
1 handful of basil sprigs
1 handful of parsley sprigs, including the stalks
2 tablespoons olive oil or unsalted butter
1 cup sunflower oil
1 pound spaghettini
kosher salt and freshly ground black pepper
3 tablespoons freshly grated Parmesan cheese, plus extra shavings, to serve

Put the eggplant in a colander and sprinkle with salt. Cover with a plate and weight it down. Put the colander over a bowl and leave to stand 1 hour to drain out the bitter juices.

Meanwhile, put the tomatoes, vegetables and herbs in a saucepan over low heat, cover and simmer very gently in their own juices until pulpy, about 30 minutes. Leave to cool, then push the mixture through a food mill or strainer into a clean, large saucepan. Alternatively, whiz together in a food processor, then push through a strainer into a large saucepan.

Put the pan over medium heat and cook the tomato sauce 15 minutes, stirring occasionally, or until it reduces and thickens. Remove the pan from the heat and stir in the olive oil or butter, then season with salt and pepper. Cover and keep warm.

While the tomato sauce is cooking, rinse the eggplant well and pat dry with paper towels. Heat the sunflower oil in a large skillet. Add the eggplant and fry 10 minutes, or until brown and lightly caramelized. Drain well on paper towels and keep warm.

Meanwhile, bring a large saucepan of salted water to a boil. Add the pasta and cook according to the package directions until al dente, then drain and return to the pan. Add the tomato sauce and toss together, then add the eggplant cubes and toss again. Stir the grated Parmesan into the pasta and serve topped with the Parmesan shavings.

CHICKPEA FARINATA

This was something that Andreina used to buy for us at the pizzeria as a snack,
after shopping at the market. It is a type of thick "pancake" with a fragrant
and creamy interior and delicious crispy edges. We would eat it out of brown
paper, scalding hot and flavored with just a little black pepper. If she made
it at home, Andreina would wrap it, piping hot, around big, very cold blobs
of *stracchino*, a sour, stretchy curd cheese that I just adore. This recipe makes
a sheet of farinata about 1¼ inches thick.

> *Serves 4*
> *Preparation time:* 15 minutes,
>   plus 1 hour standing
> *Cooking time:* 30 minutes
>
> 1½ cups chickpea flour (gram flour)
> ¼ cup olive oil
> kosher salt and freshly ground
>   black pepper

Put the chickpea flour and 6½ cups water in a large bowl and mix together thoroughly.
Season with salt and pepper, then add half the oil and leave to stand 1 hour.

Heat the oven to 400°F and grease a large, shallow baking tray (a copper baking tray
is traditionally used) with the remaining oil. Pour in the batter in an even layer, then bake
30 minutes, or until crisp on the outside but still soft in the middle. Serve hot or cold,
cut into wedges.

TORTA DI RISO

I have tried hard to recreate Giulia's wonderful rice cake without her recipe, trying to recall from memory how she made it. Yellow and rich, and deliciously moist and sticky, it contains, among other things, a generous amount of brandy. Do not use a loose-bottomed cake pan for this recipe or the liquid will ooze out.

Serves 8
Preparation time: 30 minutes
Cooking time: about 1 hour

¾ cup short-grain or pudding rice
5½ cups milk
1 small strip of unwaxed lemon peel, plus finely grated zest of ½ unwaxed lemon

2 tablespoons unsalted butter, softened
2 tablespoons semolina
8 eggs
1¼ cups sugar
3 tablespoons brandy

Put the rice, about two-thirds of the milk and the strip of lemon peel in a saucepan and bring to a boil, then boil 12 minutes until the rice is tender. Drain and discard the lemon peel. Leave the rice to cool slightly.

Heat the oven to 350°F. Grease a deep 10-inch cake pan generously with the butter, then sprinkle with the semolina to coat the base and sides. Turn the pan upside down and tap to remove any excess semolina.

Meanwhile, whisk the eggs in a mixing bowl with an electric hand-held mixer on medium speed about 15 minutes until thick and pale yellow. Add the sugar gradually, whisking continuously, then add the brandy. Stir in the lemon zest, rice and all the remaining milk.

Pour the mixture into the prepared pan and bake 50 minutes, or until golden brown and a skewer inserted in the middle comes out clean. Serve warm or cold.

Clockwise from top right, Dad, Eileen
(my father's secretary), Aunt Leonora, my
cousin Michael and my brother Gerard.

17. AT SCHOOL WITH
la Signora Leonora

My Aunt Leonora (or Leo) was one of the most remarkably elegant women I have ever met in my life. She was my father's older sister, and arrived in Rome to take up permanent residence when I was just a little girl. Her husband, Bill Warhurst, a photographer for *The Times* (of London), had died and her two sons were grown. She was alone, and obviously ready for a new challenge. I remain entranced by Aunt Leonora to this day: amazed by her ability to charm and entertain everybody around her; riveted by the way she smoked sixty cigarettes a day and chucked back neat Scotch with handfuls of prescription pills; and stunned by the outfits she wore with her own inimitable panache.

After my father sold St. George's English School of Rome in 1963, which he had set up with the purpose of educating my brothers Steve, Nick and Howard before they were dispatched to a boarding school in England, there was a slight hiatus in my own education. I was too young to be sent away to England and had already completed kindergarten at St. George's. The hiatus lasted only a few months before my father, with typical entrepreneurial spirit, decided that the best way for Leonora to get over her husband's death would be to move to Italy. There she would open another school, which I could then conveniently attend. The fact Leonora did not have any experience of teaching or running a school did not worry my father: he was sure she would make a success of it, as there was a real need for an English school for the ex-pat community in Rome. My father was absolutely correct in his faith in Leonora's abilities (and the gap in the market), and she went on to build a highly successful, well-run establishment.

> I remain entranced by Aunt Leonora to this day: amazed by her ability to charm and entertain everybody around her...

When Signora Leonora's Junior English School of Rome first opened in the early 1960s, Rome was just easing into "*la dolce vita.*" The school was housed in a lovely, secluded old villa on Via Appia Antica, which was reached via a succession of long dirt tracks and an impressive ancient brick archway.

Each day I traveled from my home at the other end of the city, passing the Coliseum, Caracalla's baths and Nero's tomb, and going through the ancient Porta Ardeatina. The final leg took me past the catacombs of San Sebastiano, the tomb of Cecilia Metella and a succession of luxurious, hidden villas. Endless archaeological remains lay scattered under vast pine trees. Only now does the privilege of those journeys almost overwhelm me.

My first few months at Signora Leonora's Junior English School of Rome consisted of me and one or two other early recruits, rattling around the building, in the charge of several teachers my aunt had employed through *The Times Educational Supplement*. In neat school uniforms of burgundy and gray, we learned to read and write with Peter and Jane. The domestic staff, including the school cook, were relatives of the staff of St. George's, and they prepared delicious, very un-English school meals. We ate colorful, vegetable-rich minestrone, pasta with tomato sauce, fried squid, succulent meatballs and my own favorite: chocolate salame, made with cocoa powder blended into a thick paste and studded with crumbled cookies and chilled until firm.

In the beginning, Leo was there every single day, and then spending her evenings busily networking her way around Rome in a valiant mission to increase the roll call. As far as I know, she had never had a "proper" job before, other than driving an ambulance in World War II and a stint working for Molyneux naming lipstick colors in an office in South Molton Street, London—an image that I have always found incredibly glamorous: I imagine Leo sitting there examining the colors and thinking up names like Flamingo Sunset or Red Berry Sky.

Leonora lived in a wonderful rooftop apartment overlooking the Coliseum. Somehow, through one of her many contacts, she had arranged for a fleet of black limousines to be our school buses, which ferried the children for the first year or so, before the school's numbers swelled thanks to Leo's networking skills at embassy parties. Often she would drive me home at the end of the school day in her sporty little Lancia Fulvia. She drove ridiculously fast, cigarette clamped between her lips, always talking nonstop.

When we reached her apartment, she would cook for me: real English food, like oxtail soup out of a can, Kedgeree (see page 205) or a chicken-and-mushroom potpie topped with her deliciously buttery pastry. I remember her voice rambling on and on, cigarette smoke curling blue. I loved to listen to

Miss Cunningham with me (pictured third from left in the back row) and my classmates.

her, chattering about her life and adventures, but my father would be driven mad by Leo's incessant talking when she came to visit. I guess he must have heard her stories—about the elegant tennis parties she used to attend at her local club, the dangerous moments at the wheel of a wartime ambulance and her beloved Scottie dog, Max—too many times before. But as far as I was concerned, she could not tell them often enough.

> I have never experienced anywhere else the almost brutal crunchiness of the bread, with its forgiving, deep, soft white middle...

Years later, when we had both moved to London, I would visit Leonora in Ealing, a west London suburb. She would cook for me again and the tastes triggered all the memories of evenings spent watching the sunset over the Coliseum. In Rome, her pies and other English meals, such as broiled lamb chops with mint sauce and apple crumble and custard sauce, had managed to taste both exotic and comforting at the same time.

At Leonora's school, lunchtimes were eagerly anticipated and there was always something wonderful to eat. I have never quite been able to recreate the perfection of the tiny squares of potatoes, roasted in olive oil and flavored with rosemary, we were served at least once a week; or the sweet crispness of the grated carrot salad. And I have never experienced anywhere else the almost brutal crunchiness of the bread, with its forgiving, deep, soft white middle that was perfect for soaking up the juices left on our plates. Only once, I recall, was there a meal that nobody could eat: *trippa alla Romana*, a perfect example of one of the many variety-meat dishes beloved by Romans for centuries. It was universally disliked by the ex-pat pupils and teachers, who sat mutely, staring at their plates, much to the annoyance and disappointment of the school cook who had obviously put her heart and soul into its preparation.

Our sporting activities—netball, athletics and cross-country running— kept us all very fit, and it was a great way to build unity between all the different nationalities that made up our school. In the summer months, swimming was added to the curriculum. I will never forget the first school swimming gala. The nearby farm had great brick tanks standing in the fields to catch rainwater. The largest tank would be scrubbed and cleaned, then filled with fresh water. With tremendous enthusiasm, we plowed up and down the water tank. There was only one obstacle: the newts, which the farmer had never managed to get rid of. Each time one of us came face to face with one of the innocent little amphibians, we would squeal.

At school, Auntie Leo was known as Mrs. Warhurst, owner, and very much the boss. I was often summoned to her office to be ticked off severely for some misdemeanor or other. I was always being caught on next door's farm, feeding the pigs or the chickens instead of being in lessons, or wandering off in the sunshine across the surrounding fields of gently waving wild barley to pick wild flowers and then losing all track of time. Later, driving home together, I could tell Leo all about my adventure with no fear of arousing the wrath she had rained down on me only hours before.

Leo's clothes—always one of the most striking things about her—were, I think, one of the many reasons she loved Rome so much. Her favorite store was called Albertina, an ultra-chic knitwear boutique at the top end of the Via Veneto, near the Café de Paris. She and my mother would go and get themselves kitted out in matching, thickly knitted tunic dresses and jackets, in emerald green or peacock blue, made to measure and very elegant. Leonora reveled in gold or silver lamé, which she wore to many of the parties she attended, and slinky long dresses, often topped off by a multicolored Pucci silk turban. Even at seventy-five, she was incredibly glamorous. Added to this, she was a tremendous flirt and good fun: she liked a drink and did not care who knew it. She became an institution all of her own—La Signora Leonora.

The school soon filled up and expanded, providing an education that extended far beyond the classroom for the sons and daughters of diplomatic families, corporate parents, movie stars, Anglo/ American Italians and many others. It was amazing to be surrounded by so many different cultures and nationalities, to go to after-school meals with friends and be served

> ... she was a tremendous flirt and good fun: she liked a drink and did not care who knew it... La Signora Leonora.

Norwegian brown cheese, Indonesian *nasi goreng* or spicy Indian curry dishes. The only sadness was many of my friends moved on after one or two years, when their parents were relocated. Even so, the memories of this happiest of times are still so vivid.

BREADED SCALLOPS WITH·TOMATO SALSA & ROAST POTATOES

Recently, I have been lucky enough to reconnect with many old friends from my schooldays and many remember scallops being their favorite school lunch.

Serves 4
Preparation time: 40 minutes,
   plus 2 hours standing
Cooking time: 30 to 40 minutes

8 thin veal, chicken or turkey scallops,
   trimmed of fat
3 eggs
3 cups fine dry bread crumbs
½ cup sunflower oil, plus extra as
   needed
kosher salt and freshly ground
   black pepper

Roast potatoes:
3½ cups baby new potatoes, peeled
   or unpeeled and cut into
   1-inch cubes
8 garlic cloves, lightly crushed
1 unwaxed lemon, cut into 8 pieces
juice of ½ lemon
2 rosemary sprigs, broken into pieces
½ cup extra virgin olive oil

Tomato salsa:
4 large, ripe tomatoes, chopped
¼ cup extra virgin olive oil
1 handful of basil leaves, torn

Put the scallops between two sheets of plastic wrap and flatten with a meat mallet or rolling pin until ¼ inch thick. Beat the eggs in a large, shallow dish. Lay the scallops in the egg, cover and chill 2 hours. Put the potatoes in a bowl of cold water and leave 2 hours.

Heat the oven to 400°F. Rinse and drain the potatoes, then pat dry in a clean tea towel. Put them in a roasting pan and add the garlic, lemon, lemon juice and rosemary. Season with salt and pepper, then mix together with your hands. Add the oil and mix again until the potatoes are well coated. Roast 30 to 40 minutes until crisp and golden brown.

Meanwhile, make the salsa. Put the tomatoes in a strainer over a bowl and leave them to drain 15 minutes. Transfer them to a clean bowl and combine with the olive oil and basil, then season with salt. Leave to one side.

Put the bread crumbs on a large plate. Drain the scallops, allowing the excess egg to drip off, then coat in the bread crumbs. Heat the sunflower oil in a large skillet over medium heat, then, working in batches, fry the scallops 4 minutes on each side, or until golden and cooked through. Add more oil, if necessary. Drain on paper towels, then season the scallops with salt and pepper and spoon the tomato salsa over. Serve with the roast potatoes.

LEO'S KEDGEREE

My Aunt Leonora (Leo) loved her classic English dishes and would often make kedgeree for me as a supper dish after school. Smoked haddock was impossible to find in Rome, so she would use smoked salmon instead, mixed in with whiting or sea bass.

Serves 4
Preparation time: 20 minutes
Cooking time: 30 minutes

¾ cup long-grain rice
4 large eggs
1 pound smoked haddock,
  or a mixture of white fish fillets
  and smoked fish
7 ounces milk
¼ cup unsalted butter

2 large onions, thinly sliced
6 cardamom pods, split
2 bay leaves
4 teaspoons curry powder
juice of ½ lemon
kosher salt and freshly ground
  black pepper
2 tablespoons finely chopped parsley
  leaves and 8 lemon wedges, to serve

Bring a large saucepan of salted water to a boil. Add the rice and bring back to a boil, then reduce the heat and simmer gently 12 to 15 minutes until tender. Drain, then return the rice to the pan, cover and leave to one side.

Meanwhile, bring a small pan of water to a boil. Add the eggs and boil 10 minutes, then drain and leave to stand until cool enough to handle.

While the rice and eggs are cooking, put the fish in a large, deep skillet and pour the milk over (add a little boiling water to cover, if necessary). Bring the milk to a boil, then reduce the heat and simmer, uncovered, 6 minutes, or until the fish turns opaque. Remove the fish with a slotted spoon, discard any skin and bones and flake into large chunks. Leave to one side, covered with foil. Discard the cooking liquid.

Melt the butter in the cleaned skillet over medium-low heat. Add the onions, cardamom pods and bay leaves, cover and sauté gently 10 minutes until the onions are soft. Add the curry powder and cook 2 minutes longer. Add the cooked rice to the onion mixture, stir well and heat through. Gently fold in the fish using a fork. Shell and quarter the eggs, reserving 4 quarters, then gently stir the remaining eggs into the rice. Add the lemon juice and season with salt and pepper. Discard the cardamom pods and bay leaves, then serve the kedgeree sprinkled with parsley and topped with the reserved egg quarters and lemon wedges.

BAKED RICE-STUFFED TOMATOES

This is similar to one of the dishes that we were served as an appetizer at school and it is perfect for large numbers, because the tomatoes can be baked together in large trays. The secret is to let the tomatoes bake gently until they are soft, sweet and sticky. They are always best if made a day in advance, and then reheated if you prefer to serve them hot.

Serves 6
Preparation time: 20 minutes,
  plus 30 minutes standing
Cooking time: 50 minutes

⅓ cup olive oil, plus extra for greasing
  and 2 tablespoons for drizzling
6 large ripe but firm tomatoes
2 garlic cloves, finely chopped

1 handful of basil leaves, torn into
  shreds
1 tablespoon dried oregano
⅔ cup long-grain rice
1 large potato, cut into 6 thick slices
kosher salt and freshly ground
  black pepper

Heat the oven to 325°F and lightly grease a baking dish with oil. Slice the tops off the tomatoes and leave to one side. Scoop out the insides of the tomatoes and discard the seeds but reserve the flesh. Turn the tomato shells upside down and leave to drain on a baking tray 30 minutes. Chop the tomato flesh, transfer it to a bowl and leave to one side.

Heat the oil in a large skillet over low heat. Add the garlic and fry 5 minutes, or until soft, then stir in the basil and oregano. Mix in the rice and the reserved tomato flesh and drained juices. Season with salt and pepper.

Fill the tomato shells two-thirds full with the rice mixture, then top with the lids. Put the tomatoes in the greased dish and tuck the potato slices in and around the tomatoes to help them stand upright. Drizzle with the 2 tablespoons oil and sprinkle with about ¼ cup water.

Bake the tomatoes 45 minutes, basting occasionally with the juices and adding more water, if necessary, to soften the rice, or until the rice is tender and the tomatoes are soft and starting to split. Serve hot or cold.

APPLE FRITTERS

We used to be served these fritters at school for dessert on cold fall days—piles and piles of them, dished out with a huge smile and plenty of sugar sprinkled on top! The Italian apple of choice for fritters is the Renetta, or Russet apple, as it is firm and crisp, and has the right balance of tart and sweetness. Any remaining batter can be dropped into the oil to fry in squiggly shapes until just golden, then drained and dusted with confectioners' sugar to be enjoyed as an extra treat.

Serves 4
Preparation time: 30 minutes
Cooking time: 30 minutes

3 large apples, such as Russet or Fuji, peeled, cored and cut into round slices
juice of ½ lemon
4½ cups sunflower oil
confectioners' sugar, for dusting

Batter:
2 eggs, separated
a pinch of salt
grated zest of ½ unwaxed lemon
⅔ cup all-purpose flour, sifted
⅓ cup milk
1 teaspoon baking powder

Lay the apples slices in a large, nonmetallic dish and sprinkle with the lemon juice to prevent them browning.

To make the batter, beat together the egg yolks, salt and lemon zest in a mixing bowl until pale and fluffy. Using a metal spoon, gradually fold in the flour, alternating with the milk, then stir in the baking powder. In a separate bowl, whisk the egg whites until soft peaks form, then gently fold them into the batter mixture.

Heat the oven to 200°F. Heat the oil in a large, deep saucepan until a small cube of bread dropped into the oil sizzles instantly. Dip the apple slices into the batter, then working in batches, drop them into the hot oil and fry 3 to 4 minutes until puffy and golden brown, turning them over once.

Remove the fritters from the pan using a slotted spoon and drain well on paper towels. Keep the fritters warm in the oven and continue frying until all the apples are cooked. Serve the apple fritters dusted with confectioners' sugar.

Largo Spinelli 15, our apartment in Rome.

18. *Italia*
THE COOK (AND HER SISTER AMERICA)

Our home in Rome, from the early 1960s to the late 1970s, was an elegant, sunny two-storey penthouse at Largo Spinelli 15, in a residential area in the middle of the city where all the streets are named after Italian composers. The top floor was surrounded by a wide terrace, tiled with terracotta and framed by countless flowerpots and plant containers, lovingly tended by my father. From it, the view across the dark green treetops of Villa Borghese stretched to the cupola of the Basilica of St. Peter on the far horizon. I lived there, with my family, until I left home for the thrills of London at the age of eighteen.

As my elementary school on the Via Appia Antica and, subsequently, my secondary school on the Via Cassia were both about 90 minutes away by bus, and none of my friends seemed to live anywhere nearby, I often felt lonely when I got home from school, even if my parents were there. Learning to cook was my way of keeping occupied once homework was done and I was bored of playing with my dolls or reading. I loved books, and was encouraged to read anything and everything by my mother, whose philosophy was that this was the only way to learn to distinguish good literature from bad. I also read a lot of recipe books, of which there was no shortage, and started to learn a great deal about food.

Despite the fact that my mother did not work, we had a lot of staff to help run the household. There was tiny, ancient little Giuseppina, who came twice a week to do all the washing by hand, her huge, gnarled, red hands out of all proportion with her bird-like body. There was Maria the maid who cleaned and ironed; Jack the ex-army chauffeur and handyman; and my favorite—the stout, sensible cook: Italia.

> **Learning to cook was my way of keeping occupied once homework was done and I was bored of playing with my dolls or reading.**

Italia came from the region of Abruzzi that has always been famous for producing great cooks. In Italy, they say that if you have an Abruzzese in your kitchen, your restaurant simply cannot fail. The Abruzzesi are renowned for their ability to season their food perfectly, and are supposed to be naturally instinctive cooks, which are always the very best kind.

Italia's repertoire of lunch dishes, which she prepared every day of the week except Sunday, was not very wide. She would do the shopping in the market on Via Metauro on her way to work and, if I was not at school, her arrival was one of the most thrilling parts of my day. Within minutes of unpacking her shopping cart, the kitchen surfaces would be covered in all kinds of fresh produce: great bunches of cardoons; live *vongole* in the sink, squirting seawater everywhere; or chunks of meat—ready to be passed through the gleaming meat grinder clamped securely to the edge of the table —which ended up as delicious little meatballs: Italia's famous *polpette*.

Unfortunately, Italia's working hours meant she was always gone by the time I returned home after school. But on Saturday mornings and during vacations, I would spend as much time as I could helping her: learning to make feather-light gnocchi on Thursdays; fish stews on Fridays; and preparing dishes that could be reheated for our family suppers in the evening, once Italia had gone home on the 39 bus to the apartment she shared with her sister, America, in the San Giovanni district of the city.

I loved to hear Italia talk of the remote village in the Abruzzo where she and her sister had been raised; and how they had been taught to make fresh pasta by their mother as soon as they reached puberty. She believed wholeheartedly that it would help them develop a good bust; and that a girl who could make excellent pasta, and had a nice firm bust with a deep cleavage, should have no trouble catching herself a husband.

"Courage!" Italia would cry, as I tried to wield the meter-long rolling pin covered in flour. "It will be worth all your effort if you just keep going!" She would flip over the disk of rolled-out, bright yellow pasta, forcing it to stretch out over and over again under the even pressure of her rolling pin, until it was fine enough "to read your love letters through it," and as silky as "your lover's caresses." I tried hard to emulate her effortless movements, but often ended up with huge holes and gaping tears in my own sheet of dough.

I laughed about her sister's name, until Italia told me that in choosing the girls' names her parents had honored both their home country and that which they considered to be the land of golden opportunities, in the hope this would guarantee good fortune and a better life than they would have in their tiny mountain village. "Life was so hard when my sister and I were growing up," she would sigh. "You are a very lucky girl to have such a wonderful life and so many lovely things, but always remember that your good health is the most important of all." So saying, she would touch my cheek and smile before pushing me gently toward the table again. "Now, try and roll out the pasta more evenly this time!"

Sometimes, my mother would take me to our local market, the one where Italia shopped every day and where everybody knew her name. In wintertime, the market traders fascinated me: bulky with the old newspapers they wrapped around themselves, worn underneath their clothes to keep out the bitter cold. The traders would yell out their prices and the provenance of their goods in the thickest of local dialects, peppered with coarse innuendoes. "Come on Signora!" they would shout at my mother. "Take home some of my blood oranges. They'll bring Sicily into your bed. Hot like a lover's kiss!" Or: "You need to fill your man's stomach if you know what's good for you, ladies! Try making your gnocchi with my potatoes: they'll be so light, he'll never stop showing you how much he loves you!"

It was such a thrill to be at the market, to see the boxes of fish and the mountains of fresh, seasonal fruit and vegetables everywhere: knobbly tomatoes and gleaming purple eggplants in the summer; heaps of wrinkle-leafed spinach and Swiss chard in the winter; shiny black mussels in vast buckets; spiny bunches of artichokes, piled high and enormous; and leafy, thick-skinned Amalfi lemons. "*Buono buono, fresco fresco!*" the vendors would call. The smells and sounds of the place filled my heart and my head to overflowing. It was the start of a lifelong obsession with markets, and I have never been able to resist them since.

On Sundays in Rome—when we were not in the country on one of my parents' epic picnics, which involved much outdoor cooking followed by hunks of bread and chocolate—my mother would take over the kitchen. Then our diet changed completely and, instead of the strong, garlic-infused southern Italian flavors that were Italia's specialties, my mother would cook English food to please my dad, or classic French dishes to please herself. Fiammetta was a dab hand not only at dishes like *gratin dauphinois*, *quiche Lorraine* and *tarte fine aux pommes* (apple tart), but also steak and kidney pie. She would make rich, deeply flavored, perfectly clear consommé: liquid and steaming hot in winter or gelled and cool in summer. She also taught me how to bake as she had learned to do while in the United States, and together we churned out endless angel food cakes, chocolate brownies, devil's food cakes, key lime pies (made with lemons because limes were unavailable in Rome back then) and icebox cookies.

One very sad day when I was about eleven, Italia told my parents that she was retiring to her village in the Abruzzi with her sister. I was devastated by the news: Italia had taught me so many things about cooking that I would treasure forever, and I couldn't imagine what life would be like without her repertoire of dishes marking the days of our week. Like Beppino, her cooking had been a great influence upon me; their style was very different from one another, but I always managed to keep the two separate in my head.

> Italia had taught me so many things about cooking... Like Beppino, her cooking had been a great influence upon me.

I had always hoped that I would get to see Italia's village one day and meet the famous America, but this was not to be. She simply stopped coming to our flat, and we heard from her only at Christmas when she sent us her traditional Abruzzese version of a strudel (see page 225), a marvelously sticky, very nutty confection of which she was terribly proud. Over time, it became as much a part of our Christmas as panettone, and the Christmas crackers my father would go to inordinate lengths to supply.

I missed Italia desperately when she left us. I still think of her from time to time, especially when I am making her feather-light Potato Gnocchi (see page 220), which she said had to be as light and small as a cherub's fart! We would make them together, peeling the boiling-hot potatoes as soon as they were drained to prevent them from absorbing too much moisture, then pushing them through a food mill three times before blending in only as much egg and flour as was needed to get them to hold their shape and retain their lightness. Once she had tested the dough, Italia would race through the cutting and shaping, pressing the little nuggets against the back of a fork or a cheese grater, while I followed her lead more cautiously.

So many of Italia's dishes are now part of my own repertoire. I doubt either of us suspected for a moment that things would turn out like this: with some of her best-loved recipes in a chapter dedicated to her memory.

Top, the view from our
penthouse flat over the
Borghese Gardens to the
Basilica of St. Peter.
Left me on the terrace.

CHICKEN WITH OLIVES
& RED PEPPERS

This is a version of one of Italia's favorite chicken recipes that we used to have for lunch at least twice a month, in some form or another. It's delicious and still makes me think of her with huge affection and a longing to taste it the way she made it. She liked to serve it with potatoes, boiled and drizzled with olive oil, then sprinkled with parsley, but I also liked it with mashed potatoes, as I've suggested here.

Serves 4
Preparation time: 20 minutes
Cooking time: 50 minutes

1¼ pounds ripe tomatoes
⅓ cup olive oil
2¾ pounds chicken pieces
3 garlic cloves, chopped
2 celery sticks, finely chopped
2 red bell peppers, halved, seeded
  and cut into large cubes

scant ½ cup white wine
1⅔ cups pitted black or green olives
1 cup chicken stock, hot
1 tablespoon roughly chopped basil
kosher salt and freshly ground
  black pepper
mashed potatoes, to serve (optional)

Cut a cross in the bottom of each tomato, using a sharp knife, then put them in a heatproof bowl and cover with boiling water. Leave to stand 2 to 3 minutes, then drain. Peel off and discard the skins, then seed and roughly chop the flesh. Leave to one side.

Heat half the oil in a large skillet over medium-high heat. Add the chicken pieces and cook until brown all over. Remove the pieces from the pan and leave to one side.

Pour the remaining oil into the pan. Add the garlic, celery and red peppers and fry about 5 minutes, stirring frequently, then return the chicken to the pan. Pour in the wine and cook 5 minutes longer, then stir in the olives and tomatoes.

Pour in about half the chicken stock, season with salt and pepper and cover. Reduce the heat and simmer 35 minutes, stirring occasionally and adding more stock, if necessary, or until the chicken is tender and the juices run clear when the thickest part of the meat is pierced with the tip of a sharp knife. Sprinkle the basil over the top and serve hot with mashed potatoes, if liked.

SQUID & PEA STEW

This dish, which Italia often used to serve on Fridays, can also be made using cuttlefish or octopus. Traditionally, very small, young and tender seafood is used, but larger squid, cuttlefish or octopus can simply be cut to size as required. Don't worry if you need to cook it for a bit longer (adding a little water or fish stock, if necessary); trust me, the squid will become tender in time.

Serves 4 to 6
Preparation time: 15 minutes
Cooking time: 1 hour

1 pound 10 ounces dressed and
   prepared squid or cuttlefish, cut
   into thick strips
⅓ cup olive oil
1½ tablespoons white wine vinegar
1½ cups fresh or frozen peas, thawed
   if frozen
1¼ cups passata or tomato puree
juice of ½ lemon
kosher salt and freshly ground
   black pepper
2 tablespoons chopped parsley leaves
lemon wedges and steamed rice,
   mashed potatoes or soft polenta,
   to serve

Put the squid, oil and vinegar in a large skillet over medium heat and cook 15 minutes, stirring occasionally, or until the liquid evaporates.

Reduce the heat, add the peas and passata and simmer 40 to 45 minutes longer until the squid is completely tender. Season with salt and pepper, then stir in the lemon juice.

Sprinkle the parsley over the stew and serve with wedges of lemon, steamed rice, mashed potatoes or soft polenta.

POTATO GNOCCHI

Italia and I would make hundreds of gnocchi, laying them out—perfectly
concave and lightly dusted with flour—on a wooden table in long rows.
It is difficult to make good gnocchi: Italia's best tip was to test a small amount
of the dough before cutting and shaping the remaining gnocchi. You might not
need as much egg or flour as specified in the recipe. Allow twelve to fourteen
gnocchi per person for a generous serving.

Serves 4

Preparation time: 1 hour, plus making
the sauce
Cooking time: about 35 minutes

2¼ pounds Idaho potatoes, unpeeled
and left whole
3 eggs, beaten

2 cups all-purpose flour, sifted
kosher salt
1 recipe quantity Italia's Rich Tomato
Sauce (see page 224), hot, and
freshly grated Parmesan cheese,
to serve

Put the potatoes in a large, heavy-based saucepan, cover with water and bring to a boil. Boil
15 to 20 minutes until just tender, then drain. Holding the potatoes in a dish towel, peel off
the skins and press the flesh through a potato ricer into a large bowl, then press through the
ricer again. Gradually add the eggs and flour and season with salt, then gently combine into a
soft dough with your hands; add as little flour as you can by checking if the dough
can hold a gnocchi shape as you work, but avoid overhandling it or the gnocchi will be tough.

Bring a small saucepan of salted water to a boil. To test that the dough is the correct
consistency, roll out a small piece on a lightly floured work surface to form a cylinder about
1½ to 2 inches thick, then cut into 1¼-inch pieces. Pinch each piece into a small, concave
gnocchi shape, pressing it against the back of a fork or a classic Parmesan grater to make
grooves on the opposite side. Drop the gnocchi into the boiling water—they should float
to the surface in about 1 minute, hold their shape without breaking and taste light and
flavorsome. If they do not, adjust the remaining dough by adding more egg, flour or both, and
add a little more salt, if needed. Continue testing until the correct texture is achieved.

Roll out the remaining dough into cylinders, then cut into pieces and shape into gnocchi as
above. Spread them out on a large, lightly floured board as you work. Bring a large saucepan
of salted water to a boil. Working in batches, drop in 8 to 10 gnocchi at a time and cook until
they float to the surface of the water, about 1 minute. Scoop them out with a slotted spoon
and keep warm. Continue until all the gnocchi are cooked. Spoon the Rich Tomato Sauce over
the gnocchi and serve sprinkled with grated Parmesan.

ROMAN SEMOLINA GNOCCHI WITH GORGONZOLA

This is one of Italia's classic dishes. As a child, cutting out the circles of semolina was one of my favorite kitchen duties. This type of gnocchi is quicker and much easier to make than potato gnocchi.

Serves 4
Preparation time: 20 minutes
Cooking time: about 30 minutes

4½ cups milk
2 cups semolina
2 egg yolks
1 cup freshly grated Parmesan cheese

scant ½ cup unsalted butter
a pinch of freshly grated nutmeg
3½ ounces Gorgonzola cheese, rind
    removed and cubed
kosher salt and freshly ground
    black pepper

Heat the oven to 425°F. Pour the milk into a large saucepan and bring to a boil. Sprinkle in the semolina so it falls like rain into the water, whisking continuously to prevent lumps forming. Continue whisking until the mixture begins to thicken, then use a wooden spoon to stir constantly 10 minutes longer, or until the mixture comes away from the sides and base of the pan and forms a soft ball.

Remove the pan from the heat, stir in the egg yolks, half the Parmesan and half the butter, then season with the nutmeg, salt and pepper.

Lightly dampen a work surface with cold water. Transfer the semolina onto the surface and, using a metal spatula dipped in water, spread out the mixture until about ½ inch thick. Stamp out circles using a 2- to 3-inch cookie cutter or upturned tumbler, wetting the edge of the cutter and your hands with a little cold water.

Grease a shallow baking dish that is suitable to serve from with a little of the remaining butter, then put a layer of scraps from the cut-out semolina on the bottom of the dish. Cover with a little grated Parmesan, a few dots of butter and half the Gorgonzola, then cover with a layer of slightly overlapping semolina circles. Repeat until all the ingredients are used.

Melt any remaining butter and trickle it over the top, then bake 15 minutes, or until golden and bubbling.

ROMAN BRAISED ARTICHOKES

This delicious way of serving artichokes is typical of the cooking style of Rome, with plenty of strong, robust flavors, such as garlic, lemon and mint. I learned about taming artichokes from Italia, and still enjoy the lengthy preparation of this magnificent vegetable almost as much as I enjoy eating it. Take your time over this because you don't want to leave any of the sharp ends on the leaves or even a small amount of the hairy choke. You might be shocked by how much waste is involved, but you must be ruthless.

Serves 4
Preparation time: 1 hour
Cooking time: 45 minutes

juice of 2 lemons
8 globe artichokes, stems trimmed
10 garlic cloves, thinly sliced into
  strips
1 large handful of mint leaves

pared peel of 1 unwaxed lemon,
  finely chopped
generous ⅓ cup dry white wine,
  plus extra if needed
⅓ cup olive oil
kosher salt and freshly ground
  black pepper

Fill a large bowl with cold water and stir in the lemon juice. To prepare the artichokes, carefully remove and discard all the external hard leaves, then trim the internal leaves. Scoop out and discard the hairy choke in the middle of each artichoke using a teaspoon. Put each artichoke in the acidulated water as soon as it is prepared to prevent it browning.

Remove the artichokes from the acidulated water and stand them upright in a large saucepan. Put a few slices of garlic inside each one, then tuck the mint leaves and lemon peel among the artichokes. Season with salt and pepper.

Pour in the wine, oil and generous 1 cup water, cover and bring to a boil. Reduce the heat and simmer gently 30 minutes, basting the artichokes occasionally and adding more wine or water if necessary, until they are almost tender all the way through. Turn the artichokes on their sides and cook 15 minutes longer, or until soft. Serve hot or cold with some juices from the pan spooned over the top.

ITALIA'S RICH TOMATO SAUCE

This sauce can also be made with canned tomatoes, passata or tomato puree, instead of fresh tomatoes. You can add chopped fresh herbs, but do this after the sauce has finished cooking, and do not reheat it once the butter or oil has been added. Italia's tomato sauce goes particularly well with the Potato Gnocchi (see page 220) or can be served with pasta.

Serves 4
Preparation time: 25 minutes
Cooking time: 45 to 60 minutes

18 ounces ripe tomatoes
¼ cup olive oil
1 onion, finely chopped
1 large celery stick, finely chopped
1 large carrot, finely chopped
3 tablespoons unsalted butter
   or extra virgin olive oil
kosher salt and freshly ground
   black pepper
Potato Gnocchi (see page 220),
   or pasta, to serve

Cut a cross in the bottom of each tomato, using a sharp knife, then put them in a heatproof bowl and cover with boiling water. Leave to stand 2 to 3 minutes, then drain. Peel off and discard the skins, then seed and roughly chop the flesh. Leave to one side.

Heat the oil in a heavy-based saucepan over low heat. Add the onion, celery and carrot and fry very gently 15 to 20 minutes until the vegetables are soft and the onion is translucent.

Stir in the tomatoes, then cover and simmer 30 to 40 minutes, stirring frequently, until the sauce reduces and thickens.

Season with salt and pepper, then remove the pan from the heat and stir in the butter or extra oil just before you are ready to serve with Potato Gnocchi or pasta.

ABRUZZESE STRUDEL

This is the famous Abruzzese version of a strudel that Italia would always make for Christmas, and then continued to send to us long after she retired as our cook in Rome.

Serves 6 to 8
Preparation time: 30 minutes,
  plus 20 minutes resting
Cooking time: 40 minutes

⅔ cup golden raisins
⅓ cup blanched almonds, chopped
8 shelled walnuts, roughly chopped
3 large apples, peeled, cored and
  sliced
5 dried figs, chopped
5 prunes, pitted and chopped

2 to 3 tablespoons confectioners'
  sugar

Pastry dough:
1¾ cups all-purpose flour, sifted, plus
  extra for dusting
½ cup sugar, plus extra for sprinkling
¼ cup extra virgin olive oil, plus extra
  for greasing
a pinch of salt

To make the pastry dough, put the flour, sugar, oil and salt in a mixing bowl and knead together, adding enough warm water to form a firm dough. Cover with a clean dish towel and leave to rest 20 minutes.

Meanwhile, put the golden raisins in a bowl, cover with warm water and soak 20 minutes, or until plump and swollen. Drain and pat dry with paper towels.

Heat the oven to 350°F. Grease a cookie sheet with oil, then dust with flour. Roll out the dough on a lightly floured work surface as thin as possible; it should be about 12 x 8 inches. Mix together the golden raisins, almonds, walnuts, apples, figs and prunes. Spoon the mixture down the middle of the dough, then sprinkle with the confectioners' sugar. Carefully roll the dough up around the filling to form a long cylinder. Wet the edge of the dough and press to seal. Sprinkle the top of the strudel with sugar.

Use 2 metal spatulas or pancake turners to transfer the strudel to the prepared cookie sheet, seam side down. Bake 40 minutes, or until crisp and golden brown. Leave to cool slightly before serving warm, or cool completely.

Top, from left my brother Gerard, Dad, my mother and Aunt Leonora. Above, my mother meeting Queen Elizabeth II.

19. LA MIA *Dolce Vita:*
EATING CAKES ON VIA VENETO

Rome in the 1960s was a wonderful place to be growing up. There was such an air of glamor everywhere. I lived in our lovely apartment by the Borghese Gardens with my parents, and went to school on the Via Appia Antica at my aunt's eccentric school. My schoolmates included the Getty family, including Paul, who was in my class. We both starred in the school production of *The Gingerbread Man* when we were six years old. He played the gingerbread man, I played the farmer's wife, and I remember I had to chase him around and around the school, shouting out, "Stop! Stop!" Unfortunately, his brown felt costume was not sewn together quite securely enough and pieces of it came adrift as he ran—until he ended up almost incapable of running at all, as he had to hold the whole costume in place with both hands to stop it falling off altogether!

My Aunt Leonora was the queen of networking and always managed to get all the most glamorous parents on the school PTA committee. The school was full of those international celebrities who were passing in and out of Rome in the sixties, which was *the* place to be in that stylish decade. When Anthony Quinn, whose children were at Leonora's school, stood up to give out prizes at one of our speech days, my classmates and I were blithely unaware that he was a well-known movie star.

With my brothers away at boarding school in England, I spent a lot of time on my own, reading or cooking in the apartment. My father, aware of my loneliness, bought me a dog—a beautiful Irish setter, Chuff. I would spend hours brushing his coat or trying to clean his teeth. He was my dearest companion and keeper of all my greatest secrets, even though he had a rather silly name. I think his Irish breeders originally spelled it is as Cheough, which I suppose is slightly more sophisticated!

> The school was full of those international celebrities who were passing in and out of Rome, which was *the* place to be in that stylish decade.

On Sunday mornings, my father and I walked Chuff across the Borghese Gardens all the way to Porta Pinciana and then down the Via Veneto to the Café de Paris. (The Via Veneto was *the* iconic symbol of 1960s Rome: a place that was to become the epicentre of *"la dolce vita,"* thanks to its numerous bars, restaurants and hotels.) We would sit down at our usual table, close to the only newsagent in the city that sold American comics and international newspapers. Our beautifully groomed, very elegant dog lay down next to us on the pavement. After my father's favorite waiter brought coffee for him and a lemon granita for me, we sat buried in an orgy of reading, enjoying the sun. I would have my nose stuck in *Casper the Friendly Ghost* or *Richie Rich*, and my dad would read his day-old *The Times* or *The Telegraph*, from London, and sometimes the *Herald Tribune*.

When we had finished, I always paused in amazement in front of the patisserie counter, marveling over the gorgeous *torta Mimosa*, *torta Saint Honoré*, *il millefoglie* and the other delicately beautiful cakes and pastries. One of my mother's cousins first told me about mimosa cake. She said the cake is made in the weeks between the mimosa blossoming in late February and vanishing again after International Women's Day. The flower has since become symbolic of International Women's Day because it was in full bloom on the first ever *Festa delle Donne* on March 8, 1946. It is customary for all women in Italy to receive bunches or sprigs of mimosa on this day, as a symbol of respect and affection. Mimosa itself is poisonous, so is not used as one of the cake's ingredients. Instead, the cake takes its name from the sponge cake crumbled over its surface, which looks remarkably like the mimosa's tiny, soft, yellow pompom flowers.

My absolute favorite cake on the patisserie counter was—and still is—the gloriously complicated *La Torta Saint Honoré* (see page 237). There is something about the little choux pastry buns I used to find completely transporting: thinly coated in crisp, transparent caramel and filled to bursting with zabaglione, sitting on top of layers of perfect sponge cake, and all sandwiched together with sweetened, whipped cream. We only ever had cakes like this for birthdays or special occasions, but I was content to just look. If I turned my attention to the glass-fronted freezer, with its display of semifreddo and ice-cream cakes, the object of my desire would always be the *Semifreddo al Torrone* (Nougat Semifreddo, see page 235), a perfect combination of creaminess and nougat crunch.

Top, my mother with my brothers Steve, Howard (Din) and Nick. Left me painting on the terrace.

One unforgettable day, the lady behind the counter called me over. She had put a huge slice of *Saint Honoré* on a plate, laid a silver cake fork next to it and beckoned me inside. It was a gift, for me! I carried it so carefully, dodging the waiters as they sped in and out of the doors, trays held high on the tips of their outstretched fingers. I sat down and gazed at my plate, trying to work out whether to eat the choux buns first, or just dive into the sponge and cream. My father lowered his newspaper and when he saw the cake he broke into a huge smile, clapped his hands and began to laugh and laugh. "Go on Vally!" he said. "I won't tell your mother you ate it just before lunch—enjoy!"

> On those occasions, I could revel in my parents' undivided attention, and would enjoy just being together.

On our way home from the café, via the same route through the gardens, my dad would tell me snippets about his wartime experiences in Rome. He painted such a lively picture of what life had been like, through a hundred anecdotes, it almost made me forget how that time had been the toughest test of his life.

"Over there," he'd say, waving a hand in the direction of the Hotel Excelsior, "we'd have such wild parties. You wouldn't believe half of what we got up to, even in those dark days!" And another time: "When I got ill with diphtheria, your mother used to bribe everyone she knew to come and visit me in the military hospital. Their visiting times were so strict, but your mother always managed to ignore that—you know what a rebel she is!"

I was proud to walk alongside my father, his huge hand engulfing mine. It felt so secure, as though nothing bad could ever happen. With him at my side, I did not think about how much I was missing my brothers, or the fact I had so few friends. I know it was a good time for my dad, too, as I rarely saw him so calm and serene.

Once home, my mother would have cooked lunch. We often had friends or family over, but some of my very favorite times were when there was nobody else coming to lunch. On those occasions, I could revel in my parents' undivided attention, and would enjoy just being together, the three of us. I sat back and basked in their love for each other, which shone out so bright and clear in their every glance.

If there was nobody else coming to lunch, my mother always made our favorite things—although, it being a Sunday, English rules were observed. The main course was always a roast, which my father carved with flair. He was especially fond of beef (My Mother's Sunday Roast Beef, see page 232), which my mother inevitably under roasted so my father complained about it being too rare. He spent ages sharpening his knife, then sliced the meat perfectly thinly. With the roast beef, scented with rosemary from a pot on the terrace, there would be buttered carrots and cabbage, and gravy, often made with a little Bisto that my mother had smuggled home from England or thickened with a brown roux, but always a big slug of red wine. Her roast potatoes were not quite as "crisp on the outside and fluffy on the inside" as my father would have liked: "These are not like the roast potatoes we have in England, are they?" he would grumble.

Dessert was a rather battered-looking apple pie, sometimes with a pitcher of hot Bird's custard, made from the canned powder variety that, like the Bisto, would be tucked into my mother's suitcase on one of our frequent visits to London. "Delicious, darling," my father would always say at the end of the meal, his hand covering my mother's on the table, "but next time, please can the beef be a little less bloody." Then he would chuckle and add, "But the gravy and custard were perfect, as usual!"

Every time my mother served apple pie she would pause before sitting down and ask me, "Are you sure you don't want ice cream with that? Like I used to have it in the States?" Something in her tone gave me the feeling I should say yes, and so I always did. It seemed so important for my mother, in the midst of all this Englishness at our table, that she should be allowed to introduce something that was her very own.

After lunch, my father rose from the table, kissed my mother tenderly, and said, "I'm off for my siesta darling, thank you so much." He never missed his afternoon nap and while he slept my mother and I played board games (we were especially fond of Cluedo and Scrabble), or read together. In warm weather, I would go up to the top terrace with its amazing view across the park, with St. Peter's in the hazy distance. There I would play with Chuff in the sunshine.

Those Sundays with my parents were magical days, precious and few, before the advent of boyfriends and my teenage social whirl swept them away in an unstoppable tide.

MY MOTHER'S SUNDAY ROAST BEEF

This is the roast beef that caused so much consternation on Sundays because my mother always cooked it very rare, the way Italians tend to like it. I have allowed seventy minutes roasting time, but you can increase or decrease this as you prefer, depending on how you like your meat cooked. Remove the meat from the refrigerator 1 hour before cooking to bring it to room temperature. Roasting the meat on a rack creates convection in the oven so you do not need to turn the roast, and the meat is placed fat-side up so as it cooks the fat melts and bathes the entire roast.

Serves 6
Preparation time: 15 minutes,
  plus 15 minutes resting
Cooking time: 1 hour 15 minutes

3½ pounds beef roast, such as sirloin
  or topside
2 garlic cloves, cut into 8 slivers
8 small rosemary sprigs
2 to 3 tablespoons olive oil
kosher salt and freshly ground
  black pepper

roast potatoes, buttered carrots and
  steamed cabbage, to serve

Gravy:
1¾ cups red wine, water or beef stock
1 tablespoon cornstarch
1 rosemary or thyme sprig (optional)

Heat the oven to 375°F. Using a sharp knife, make 8 small incisions in the beef, then push a sliver of garlic and rosemary sprig into each incision. Spread the oil all over the roast and season with salt and pepper.

Put the meat, fat side up, on a roasting rack over a roasting pan. Roast 30 minutes, or until brown, then reduce the temperature to 225°F and roast 40 minutes longer, or until the beef is cooked to your liking. Leave to rest 15 minutes, loosely covered in foil to keep it warm.

To make the gravy, put the roasting pan containing the meat juices on the stovetop over medium heat. Add the red wine and stir, scraping up the brown bits from the bottom of the pan. Mix together the cornstarch and 2 tablespoons cold water in a small bowl until smooth, then stir it into the gravy. Add a rosemary or thyme sprig, if you like, and cook until the gravy is thicker, stirring continuously to avoid lumps forming. Season with salt and pepper. Strain through a fine strainer into a gravy boat. Carve the beef into thin slices and serve with the gravy, roast potatoes, buttered carrots and cabbage.

NOUGAT SEMIFREDDO

Sometimes on my Sunday morning visits to the Café de Paris with my father, I would eschew the lemon granita I loved so much and really go for it with a semifreddo from the freezer. This one, made with ground nougat and drizzled with a stream of bitter, dark chocolate (which was usually poured from a tiny silver pitcher by a handsome waiter in white gloves), remains one of my favorite desserts in the world.

Serves 6
Preparation time: 30 minutes,
   plus 8 hours freezing and
   30 minutes standing
Cooking time: 5 minutes

7 ounces hard nougat
2 eggs, separated
3½ tablespoons sugar

2 tablespoons brandy
1 cup plus 2 tablespoons chilled
   whipping cream
4 ounces dark or unsweetened
   chocolate, broken into small pieces
1 teaspoon drinking cocoa powder,
   to serve

Line six ⅓-cup molds or a 2¼-cup loaf pan with plastic wrap. Finely chop the nougat, or put it in a food processor and whiz to a coarse powder.

Beat the egg yolks in a mixing bowl until pale, then whisk in the sugar and brandy. Gently fold in the chopped nougat. Whisk the egg whites in another bowl until soft peaks form, then whip the cream in a separate bowl until soft peaks form. Fold these alternately into the nougat mixture.

Pour the mixture into the prepared molds or pan, cover with plastic wrap and put in the freezer at least 8 hours, or until solid.

Remove the semifreddo from the freezer and leave to stand 30 minutes before serving.

Meanwhile, put the chocolate in a heatproof bowl and rest it over a pan of gently simmering water, making sure the bottom of the bowl does not touch the water. Heat 4 to 5 minutes, stirring occasionally, until the chocolate melts. Leave to cool and pour into a pitcher until ready to serve.

Turn the semifreddos out onto serving plates, or cut into slices, and drizzle with the melted chocolate. Sift a little cocoa powder over the tops and serve immediately.

LA TORTA SAINT HONORÉ

This is my "simplified" version of the masterpiece I used to so admire in the patisseries on the Via Veneto, the gloriously decadent, rich and fabulous *la torta Saint Honoré*. I have to say we never made this at home, as any attempt would never be a match for the fabulous cake available to buy from the *pasticceria*, but I decided just to have a go, and with some time and patience, you should be able to make a passable interpretation. If you like, use your own tried-and-tested favorite sponge cake recipe to make the base for this very rich and indulgent cake.

Serves 10
Preparation time: about 3 hours, plus cooling and chilling
Cooking time: about 1 hour 5 minutes

Sponge cake (makes 2):
butter, for greasing
1¾ cups all-purpose flour, plus extra for dusting
6 eggs
2 tablespoons cornstarch
1⅓ cups sugar
grated zest of 1 unwaxed lemon
2 teaspoons baking powder

Choux buns:
4½ tablespoons unsalted butter
½ cup all-purpose flour, sifted
2 eggs, beaten

Chantilly cream and caramel:
1¼ cups heavy cream
1 tablespoon confectioners' sugar
1 teaspoon vanilla extract or the seeds from ½ vanilla bean
1 tablespoon rum or Cognac (optional)
¾ cup sugar

Custard cream:
3 egg yolks
½ cup sugar
heaped ½ cup all-purpose flour, sifted
2 cups plus 2 tablespoons milk
pared peel of 1 unwaxed lemon, white pith removed
1 cup plus 2 tablespoons whipping cream
1 tablespoon confectioners' sugar
½ teaspoon vanilla extract
heaped 1 tablespoon unsweetened cocoa powder

Liqueur syrup:
¾ cup sugar
⅔ cup liqueur, such as rum, Grand Marnier or Cointreau

1¼ cups toasted, blanched hazelnuts, coarsely chopped, to decorate

First, make the sponge cakes. Heat the oven to 350°F. Grease two 9-inch cake pans with butter, then line the bottoms with wax paper and lightly flour. Beat the eggs in a mixing bowl until pale and triple in volume.

Sift the flour and cornstarch into a separate bowl, then sift again. Gradually whisk the sugar, sifted flour, lemon zest and baking powder into the eggs. Divide the batter between the prepared pans and bake 20 to 25 minutes, until a skewer inserted into the middle of each comes out clean. Leave the cakes to cool in the pans 10 minutes, then transfer them to a wire rack to cool completely.

To make the choux buns, put the butter and ½ cup cold water in a saucepan and bring to a boil over medium heat. Immediately add the flour and stir continuously with a wooden spoon. Cook a couple of minutes until the dough pulls away from the sides of the pan, forming a ball.

Put the ball of choux dough in a mixing bowl or the bowl of an electric mixer and beat for a few minutes, using a wooden spoon or the paddle attachment, until cooled slightly. Gradually add the beaten eggs in 3 or 4 additions, scraping down the side of the bowl and mixing until the dough is smooth, firm and pipeable. Transfer to a disposable pastry bag or cake syringe and chill until required.

Heat the oven to 400°F and line a large cookie sheet with parchment paper. Pipe about 10 walnut-size mounds of dough, spaced well apart, onto the cookie sheet. Bake on the middle shelf of the oven 8 to 10 minutes. Reduce the temperature to 250°F and bake 7 to 10 minutes longer until golden brown and crisp, without any unbaked dough in the middle of the buns. Transfer the choux buns to a wire rack and leave to cool.

Meanwhile, make the Chantilly cream. Whip together the cream, confectioners' sugar, vanilla extract and rum, if using, until soft peaks form. Transfer to a disposable pastry bag or cake syringe and chill at least 30 minutes.

When the choux buns are cool, snip an opening in the bottom of each one using sharp scissors, then squeeze in the cream. Leave to one side on a wire rack.

To make the caramel, put the sugar and 3 tablespoons cold water in a small, heavy-based saucepan over low heat until the sugar dissolves, stirring occasionally.

Turn the heat up to medium-high and boil the sugar syrup 10 to 15 minutes, without stirring, but occasionally swirling the mixture around the pan, until it is a golden caramel color. Half-coat each choux bun lightly in the caramel, then leave to one side on the wire rack.

To make the custard cream, beat the egg yolks in a mixing bowl until pale and foaming. Gradually beat in the sugar, then slowly add the flour and milk, stirring continuously. Add the lemon peel, pour into a saucepan and cook over low heat about 15 minutes, stirring, or until as thick as heavy cream. Pour into a heatproof bowl, discard the lemon peel and leave to cool completely.

In a separate bowl, whip the cream until stiff peaks form. Remove the skin from the top of the cooled custard and fold in the cream, confectioners' sugar and vanilla extract. Cover and chill until required.

To make the liqueur syrup, put the sugar and ⅔ cup cold water in a small, heavy-based saucepan over low heat until the sugar dissolves, stirring occasionally. Turn the heat up slightly and stir continuously until it forms a thin syrup. Leave to cool, then stir in the liqueur and leave to one side.

To assemble the cake, carefully cut the outside crusts off the sponge cakes. Scrape a little of the cake crumb out of each cake to create slight hollows; discard the cake crumb. Pour the liqueur syrup over the cakes and leave to soak.

Meanwhile, take 5 tablespoons of the custard cream and put it into a bowl, then put another 5 tablespoons in a second bowl. Stir the cocoa powder into the cream in one of the bowls until evenly blended, then cover and chill both bowls.

Spread some of the remaining custard cream over the top of one of the cakes and sandwich together with the second cake. Cover the top and sides with the remaining cream, then sprinkle the sides with the chopped hazelnuts. Arrange the choux buns on top of the cake in neat rows.

Spoon the reserved custard cream and chocolate custard cream into two separate pastry bags. Alternately pipe little mounds between the buns without covering them. Chill the cake until ready to serve.

*Top, preparing lunch for my
dollies-in my first restaurant,
Il Pino.
Right, my brother Steve and
cousin Tim.*

20. *Il Pino*:
MY FIRST RESTAURANT

When I was a little girl, standing on a chair in the kitchen of my childhood home in Tuscany, I learned to make the most perfect risotto in the world. That memory is one of pure, intense happiness and, most importantly, it is the single moment that established my future occupation. In an instant, I became immersed in the ritual, rhythm, emotion and tradition of cooking, and I have remained caught up in it ever since.

The magical house that wove the spell, La Tambura, is named after the drum-shaped mountain that stands at some distance behind it. Outings to these mountains were a part of my parents' epic picnics, which they loved to create for us when we were children. There was always a routine to be observed: first, a fire had to be built to cook on; then we would ignite the wood we had all gathered together. When the fire was ready, we would cook steaks and any fish we might have caught, or toast bread, rubbed with garlic and drizzled with olive oil, over the glowing embers. On our way home from our picnic, we would sometimes stop at a little village café to buy a snack: my favorite was *panzanella*, fragrant basil leaves wrapped in fluffy pizza dough and deep fried in piping-hot olive oil until perfectly crisp.

At home at La Tambura, we were almost self-sufficient. Thanks to Beppino's hours of work in the garden, we had all the vegetables we needed; and we made bread, caught our own fish, kept chickens, rabbits and a pig, and made our own wine (there was even a still for grappa). I grew up not just understanding where food comes from, but also taking its cycles and natural logic absolutely for granted.

I thought tomatoes would always taste sun-warmed and sweet, that everybody picked their own green beans straight from the plant and that skinning and gutting a rabbit was a completely normal thing to do.

> I thought tomatoes would always taste sun-warmed and sweet, that everybody picked their own green beans straight from the plant...

It was natural for us to talk about food, and the conversation flowed across the kitchen table, the aroma of freshly brewed espresso or simmering stock hanging between the words. I hungered to find out more, asking questions about every part of the culinary processes, about every ingredient and cooking method.

When my three big brothers came home for vacations, I would spend hours in the kitchen helping to prepare their favorite meals. The boys, who were my childhood heroes, invariably arrived with a girlfriend in tow, and very often a crowd of friends. On some mornings, during the long hot summers at La Tambura, I would wake up, fling open the heavy green shutters, and find that at least three small tents had appeared in the garden overnight. I would know at once that there would be glamorous boys at the breakfast table who had taken up my brothers' casual invitation to come and visit. Then I would tear off to the henhouse for freshly laid eggs. Knowing we had special guests, I would feed the chickens and rabbits with all sorts of extra goodies to fatten them up. I had a special, rather gruesome, treat for the chickens that involved cooking grasshoppers over an open fire on sticks until crisp. I would explain to anybody who asked that this was my way of giving the hens a nice hot meal.

Late at night, after one of their raucous drinking sessions, my brothers and their friends would make spaghetti with garlic and chili, their favorite hangover cure. They would try very hard to be quiet as they stumbled about the kitchen at 3 a.m., but I always heard them because my bedroom was directly above. I would come down in my nightie to "help" them and usually ended up eating a bowlful of my own. Their theory was that the pasta soaks up the alcohol; the chili and garlic help to purify your blood; the olive oil lines your stomach to stop the nausea; and the stink from the garlic will keep everybody away as you recover from the mighty headache the next day!

With so many mouths to feed, the kitchen was kept busy at La Tambura. I spent many hours helping my mother and Andreina, and my passion for cooking grew steadily. By the time I was eight years old, I had inaugurated my first restaurant. It was in the garden of the house, under a thatched bamboo roof over a nine-foot-square sandpit. Beppino's daughter, Rossana, and I ran this restaurant for family and friends. It had one table, one set of china and silverware, and many variations on the mud or sand pie, with an extensive grass and leaf salad range. We served our dishes with a pure white cloth draped over one arm, wrote out neat bills and were as deferential and polite as possible to all our customers (usually, my mother, taking on various roles).

When I was about ten, there came the big change from pretend to real food. My parents, with typical nonchalance, gave me several camping stoves, spare gas canisters and a large box of matches. From then on, every penny of my allowance went on buying real ingredients, and the menu at *Il Pino* (named after Beppino, of course) improved dramatically, and soon both Rossana and I could cook better than any of our friends. We were soon confident with our signature dishes: *pasta al pomodoro* (pasta with tomato sauce), *scaloppine al limone* (veal scallops with lemon) and *Bistecca alla Pizzaiola* (Steak Pizzaiola, see page 245). Almost overnight, these simple dishes replaced our sand pies and grass salads.

> **I was making food for paying customers, and I was loving it. My career as a professional cook had begun...**

We also made *pasta al burro e Parmigiano*, otherwise known as *pasta all'Inglese*. We learned to mix copious amounts of unsalted butter and freshly grated Parmesan cheese into the pasta as soon as it was drained, realizing the importance of not adding the cheese until the butter had coated the hot pasta, so it did not clump together. It is still my ultimate comfort food: a dish my family turns to in a crisis, or when they feel ill and need sustenance.

My passion for cooking never did diminish, even during my teenage years when hanging outside cafés with my friends began to fill my spare time. And when I started going out with my first boyfriend, I was still drawn to the kitchen—only this time it was his mother's, where I learned how to cook Neapolitan food. (And I have to confess that her ragu stayed in my memory far longer than he did.)

After I finished school, my parents enrolled me at the *Cordon Bleu* cooking school, in Rome. It meant they had me at home for a little longer, but they sensed once the course was finished I would want to leave Italy to test my wings. With two diplomas tucked under my arm and a head full of recipes passed down from several generations of women in my family (not to mention Italia, Beppino and Andreina), I left Rome for the restaurant kitchens of London. My little garden restaurant at La Tambura felt a long way from me now—in distance and in time. I was making food for paying customers, and I was loving it. My career as a professional cook had begun...

SAUSAGE, CHICKEN & SAGE SKEWERS

Rossana and I used to make these skewers all the time in our sandpit-cum-restaurant, raiding Beppino's herb patch for the biggest sage leaves going. Once, Beppino helped us to make them, cutting long, thick sticks of rosemary from the biggest bush, on to which we diligently threaded the chunks of chicken, sausages, bread and sage. If you can, use Italian link sausages, but those made with wild boar work well, too. We would barbecue the skewers, but you can also cook them in the oven.

Serves 6
Preparation time: 25 minutes
Cooking time: 15 to 20 minutes

3 skinless, boneless chicken breast halves, each cut into 6 pieces
2 tablespoons extra virgin olive oil, plus extra for brushing
12 crusty, thick slices of bread, cut into 1½-inch cubes

12 Italian pure pork or wild boar link sausages, halved or cut to a similar size to the chicken pieces
24 large sage leaves
kosher salt and freshly ground black pepper
sautéed potatoes and green salad, to serve

Prepare the barbecue, if using. Alternatively, heat the oven to 400°F. Put the chicken pieces in a bowl and pour the oil over. Turn the chicken until it is coated in the oil, then season with salt and pepper.

Thread the bread cubes, chicken, sausages and sage onto 6 long metal skewers, starting with a piece of bread and alternating the meat with the bread and a sage leaf. Finish with a cube of bread to hold everything in place.

Brush the skewers lightly with oil and lay them on the grill rack of a barbecue to cook 15 to 20 minutes, turning frequently and brushing with more oil, until the chicken is cooked through and the juices run clear when you pierce a piece. Alternatively, put the skewers, suspended across a roasting pan, in the oven and roast 20 minutes, or until the chicken is cooked through. Serve hot with sautéed potatoes and a green salad.

STEAK PIZZAIOLA

This is one of the first meat dishes I learned to make as a child, and I have
loved it ever since. It was part of the repetoire of dishes my best friend Rossana
and I would make at our first "restaurant"called *Il Pino* at La Tambura. This
is the most basic version of the recipe, but you can also add a few chopped
olives and/or capers to the tomato sauce if you want to add other flavors;
it can also be made with chicken, pork or even fish.

Serves 4
Preparation time: 5 minutes
Cooking time: 10 minutes

4 minute steaks, trimmed
3 tablespoons olive oil
3 garlic cloves, chopped

½ cup passata or tomato puree
heaped 1 teaspoon dry oregano
kosher salt and freshly ground
  black pepper
1 tablespoon chopped parsley leaves
  and mashed potatoes, to serve

Put the steaks between 2 sheets of plastic wrap or wax paper and flatten evenly with a meat
mallet or rolling pin until ⅝ inch thick.

Heat the oil in a large, heavy-based skillet over medium heat. Add the garlic and fry
about 3 minutes, or until just beginning to color. Stir in the passata and oregano and season
with salt and pepper.

Put the steak into the sauce and cook 4 minutes longer until just cooked through. Sprinkle
the steaks with parsley and serve with mashed potatoes.

MUSSEL & LEEK SAFFRON SOUP

This is perhaps my favorite of all the celebration dishes my mother used
to make for us. She adored mussels in a way that is hard to describe politely.
This is a refined kind of soup, which my mother learned to make during her
years in Brussels, and the boys and I subsequently enjoyed at La Tambura.

Serves 4
Preparation time: 30 minutes
Cooking time: 40 minutes

3 pounds 5 ounces mussels
2½ cups dry white wine
1 large leek, trimmed, chopped and
  rinsed, green tops kept separate
¼ cup unsalted butter

1 cup arborio rice
1¾ cups light fish stock, hot
⅛ teaspoon saffron powder
¼ cup heavy cream
sea salt and freshly ground
  black pepper
snipped chives, to serve

Scrub the mussels thoroughly with a stiff brush under cold running water to remove all traces
of grit, then remove any barnacles or other debris attached to the shells and pull off and
discard the "beards." Rinse again and discard any with broken shells or that do not close
as soon as they are tapped.

Pour the wine into a large, deep saucepan and bring to a boil over medium heat. Add the
green leek tops and mussels, cover with a tight lid and steam 6 to 8 minutes, shaking the pan
occasionally and stirring once, until the shells open. Discard any that remain closed.

Drain the mussels over a bowl, reserving the cooking liquid. Take most of the mussels out
of their shells (leaving a few in their shells to serve) and leave to one side. Discard the shells.
Strain the cooking liquid through a fine strainer into a clean saucepan and warm through
over medium heat.

Melt half the butter in a deep skillet. Add the white part of the leeks and fry until just
softened, but not colored. Stir in the rice and cook 4 to 5 minutes, then add the remaining
butter and stir in the hot cooking liquid. Add three-quarters of the fish stock, cover and
simmer gently 10 minutes, then stir in the saffron powder and the remaining fish stock and
simmer 10 minutes longer, or until the rice is tender and the soup is thick.

Stir in the mussels and heat through 1 minute, then remove the pan from the heat and stir
in the cream. Season with salt and pepper and serve sprinkled with chives.

LOBSTER BISQUE

This remains one of my favorite soups, and is such a canny way of using up every single little morsel of this superb crustacean. It holds happy memories for me: a kitchen covered in pieces of shell and my brother, Nick, lighting the Cognac and singeing one eyebrow!

Serves 4
Preparation time: 1 hour
  15 minutes
Cooking time: 45 minutes

3 cooked lobsters, about 1½ pounds
  each
¼ cup vegetable oil
2 carrots, diced
3 celery sticks, diced
5 shallots, chopped
¼ cup unsalted butter
2 tablespoons all-purpose flour

¼ cup cognac
4½ cups fish stock
1 cup dry white wine
1 tablespoon chopped tarragon leaves,
  plus extra to serve
1 cup heavy cream
1¾ cups passata or tomato puree
1 bouquet garni
a pinch of cayenne pepper
kosher salt and freshly ground
  black pepper

Remove the meat from the lobster tails, claws and body, and any roe and tomalley (liver). Remove and discard the head sac and black intestinal tract from each lobster. Put the meat in a bowl and chill. Using a mallet or a hammer, break the lobster shells into small pieces.

Heat the vegetable oil in a large saucepan over medium heat. Add the carrots, celery and shallots and fry 10 minutes, or until soft. Add the butter and the broken lobster shells and stir well. Stir in the flour and cook 2 to 3 minutes, stirring occasionally. Transfer the vegetable mixture into a bowl. Add the cognac to the pan, and either carefully flame it or let it bubble until the alcohol evaporates. Scrape any brown bits from the bottom of the pan, then return the vegetable mixture, stir, and heat through over medium-low heat 5 minutes. Add the fish stock and heat gently 5 to 10 minutes, stirring until thickened.

Add the wine, tarragon, cream, passata, bouquet garni and cayenne and simmer about 5 minutes, then pass the soup through a fine strainer or *chinois* into a clean saucepan, pressing down with the back of a ladle to squeeze out every bit of flavor. Heat the soup over low heat until just below boiling point, then add the lobster meat, tomalley and roe. Heat through until hot, season with salt and pepper and serve sprinkled with extra tarragon.

SPAGHETTI WITH GARLIC, OIL & CHILI

Yes, I know, this is a very simple recipe indeed, but I have included it because it is so evocative of those mad, happy times spent with my big brothers at La Tambura, especially at 3 a.m., when they would often make it after too much of a good night! Timing is quite crucial in this recipe, as you don't want the oil to overheat and burn the garlic or chilies, yet it must be very hot when it is tossed with the spaghetti.

Serves 4
Preparation time: 5 minutes
Cooking time: about 15 minutes

14 ounces spaghetti
scant ½ cup extra virgin olive oil
3 garlic cloves, unpeeled and left
   whole, then lightly crushed

1 or 2 dry red chilies, very lightly
   crushed
kosher salt and freshly ground
   black pepper
2 tablespoons chopped parsley leaves,
   to serve

Bring a large saucepan of salted water to a boil. Throw in the pasta and stir. Cover and return to a boil, then remove the lid and cook according to the package directions until al dente.

Meanwhile, heat the oil, garlic and chilies in a skillet over medium heat until the garlic browns slightly, but take care it doesn't burn or the oil will become bitter. Remove the garlic and chilies using a slotted spoon, then discard. Keep the oil hot.

Drain the pasta and return to the pan, then pour the hot oil over and toss together. Season with pepper, stir in the parsley and serve.

MOM'S CHOCOLATE CAKE

This was the classic cake that my mom would always make in anticipation of my brothers' return from boarding school during their vacations. As I recall, I seemed to make it more often than she did as I got older, although it never quite came out as well as when she made it for her sons.

Serves 8
Preparation time: 25 minutes,
   plus cooling
Cooking time: 50 to 55 minutes

1 stick (½ cup) unsalted butter, plus
   extra for greasing
4 ounces dark or unsweetened
   chocolate, broken into small pieces

heaped ¾ cup sugar
3 eggs, separated
2¾ cups all-purpose flour
2 teaspoons baking powder
½ teaspoon salt
⅓ cup milk
1 teaspoon vanilla extract
whipped cream, to serve

Heat the oven to 350°F and grease a deep 10-inch cake pan with butter. Put the chocolate in a heatproof bowl and rest it over a pan of gently simmering water, making sure the bottom of the bowl does not touch the water. Heat 4 to 5 minutes, stirring occasionally, until the chocolate melts. Set to one side and leave to cool.

Meanwhile, cream together the butter and sugar in a mixing bowl until light and fluffy. In a separate bowl, beat the egg yolks until pale and thick, then stir gently into the creamed butter and sugar. Stir in the cooled melted chocolate.

Sift together the flour, baking powder and salt in another bowl. Mix together the milk and vanilla extract in a measuring jug. Add the dry ingredients and the milk alternately to the chocolate mixture, beating well after each addition.

Whisk the egg whites in a clean bowl until soft peaks form, then fold them carefully into the cake batter.

Pour the batter into the greased pan and bake 45 to 50 minutes until a skewer inserted into the middle of the cake comes out clean. Leave the cake to cool in the pan 5 minutes, then turn it out onto a wire rack to cool completely. Serve with a generous spoonful of whipped cream.

RICOTTA CREAM WITH AMARETTI

Making desserts at our "restaurant" *Il Pino* was always tricky, as we did not have a refrigerator in the garden! This simple ricotta cream was something Rossana and I would make when we got bored with making fruit salad in various guises. We enjoyed beating the egg yolks until they were creamy, and used a corner of the household refrigerator to chill our dessert.

Serves 4
Preparation time: 20 minutes, plus at least 2 hours chilling

3 egg yolks
3 tablespoons ricotta cheese
2 tablespoons sugar
3 tablespoons Amaretto liqueur
4 amaretti cookies, roughly crumbled, plus extra to serve
½ cup heavy cream

Beat the egg yolks and ricotta in a mixing bowl until very pale, then beat in the sugar. Add the liqueur and amaretti cookies and gently stir together.

In a separate bowl, whip the cream until soft peaks form, then fold it into the ricotta mixture.

Spoon into small sundae dishes, espresso cups or small wine glasses and chill at least 2 hours. Serve chilled with extra crumbled amaretti cookies sprinkled over the tops.

THE CHARACTERS

The following people are all mentioned in this book, and include members of my extended family and those who have played an important part in our lives over the many years this book covers. They are listed in alphabetical order.

ANDREINA Beppino's wife, an amazing cook, incredible housekeeper and a great friend and confidante.

ANTONIO Andreina and Beppino's son, who shares the same birthday as me and gave me my first proper kiss.

BEATRICE DANIELS (TRIXIE) Sister of my grandmother, Rose.

BEPPINO The family caretaker at our house in Tuscany, La Tambura, and the man who inspired me as a child to become a professional cook.

CHUFF My glorious Irish setter, companion and keeper of all my childhood secrets.

LA COMTESSE VALENTINE ERREMBAULT DE DUDZEELE My Belgian maternal grandmother, cousin to the Belgian royal family, who married my grandfather, Count Carlo Sforza.

COUNT ALESSANDRO SFORZA Brother of my grandfather Carlo, who was kept under house arrest in the family home before being imprisoned by the SS during World War II.

COUNT ASCANIO SFORZA Brother of my great grandfather, Count Giovanni Sforza.

COUNT CARLO SFORZA My maternal grandfather, was born in 1873 in the family home in Montignoso di Lunigiana, Tuscany, and died in 1952, in Rome. He was an Italian diplomat and statesman, an exile during the Fascist era and became a major figure in post-World War II foreign affairs. My grandfather entered the diplomatic service in 1896 and served in Cairo, Paris, Constantinople (where he met and fell in love with my grandmother, Valentine), Beijing, Bucharest, Madrid, London and Belgrade. He was Undersecretary of State for Foreign Affairs from 1919–20 and Minister for Foreign Affairs from 1920–21. Appointed ambassador to France in February 1922, he resigned nine months later, refusing to serve under Mussolini.

COUNT CESARE SFORZA Brother of my great grandfather, Count Giovanni Sforza.

COUNT GASTON CHARLES ERREMBAULT DE DUDZEELE My grandmother Valentine's father.

COUNT GIOVANNI SFORZA My great grandfather, father of Carlo, who had three brothers.

COUNT GIOVANNI SFORZA (GIOVANNINO) Brother of my great grandfather, Count Giovanni Sforza.

COUNT SFORZA SFORZA (SFORZINO) My mother, Fiammetta's brother and son of Carlo and Valentine.

FIAMMETTA BIANCA MARIA SCOTT (née SFORZA) My mother, daughter of Carlo and Valentine.

GASTON ERREMBAULT DE DUDZEELE (UNCLE BOB) The younger brother of my grandmother, Valentine. He married Lili (Natalia) in Eastbourne in 1920 and they had two daughters, Helene and Anne Marie.

GERARD AND ANGELA SCOTT My half brother and sister.

GERARD SCOTT (formerly SCHOETEL) My Dutch paternal grandfather, who became a British citizen and married my Irish grandmother, Rose Daniels.

GERARD SCOTT My father's brother, first born son to Gerard and Rose.

GERMAINE ERREMBAULT DE DUDZEELE (TANTE GERMAINE) The beloved sister of my grandmother Valentine and Uncle Bob. She became the family diarist and wrote about their daily activities on practically anything she could find in her trademark violet ink.

GIULIA Andreina's mother and the "Queen of Cakes."

HOWARD (DIN) My youngest brother.

HOWARD SCOTT My father, son of Gerard and Rose.

ITALIA Our cook in Rome, who taught me how to make gnocchi among many other things, especially the cooking of her native Abruzzi. She had a sister called America.

KING ALEXANDER OF SERBIA Ruled from 1889–1903, when he and his wife, Queen Draga, were assassinated by a group of army officers led by Colonel Dragutin Dimitrijevi. When my grandmother, Valentine, danced with the king in Belgrade, in 1889, he had only recently been crowned king, and was merely thirteen years old.

LEONORA My father's sister, Aunt Leo, who moved to Rome from England to open the Junior English School of Rome, which I attended.

MARIETTO Our milkman at La Tambura.

MOLLY My cousin and Aunt Leonora's daughter-in-law. She is mother to Tim and Caroline.

NANNY MISCHA My mother and Uncle Sforzino's faithful Irish nanny.

NATALIA KONSTANTINOVIC (TANTE LILI) Married Prince Mirko Petrovi-Njegoš on July 25, 1902, to become Princess of Montenegro. Lili fell in love with my mother's Uncle Bob, but was only free to marry him once Prince Mirko had died.

NICK My middle brother.

PAULA My father's sister, Aunt Paula, who would entertain us royally at Harrods, where she ran the lighting department, whenever we visited London from Rome.

PETER My father's beloved youngest brother, who died all too soon.

PRINCE MIRKO DIMITRI PETROVI-NJEGOŠ OF MONTENEGRO, GRAND VOIVODE OF GRAHOVO AND ZETÀ Second son of King Nicholas I of Montenegro. Prince Mirko predeceased his father and his elder brother, the Crown Prince Danilo.

QUEEN ELENA OF ITALY Elena of Montenegro was the daughter of King Nicholas I of Montenegro and sister to Prince Mirko of Montenegro, who went on to marry Lili. As wife of Victor Emmanuel III of Italy, she was Queen of Italy from 1900–1946.

ROSE DANIELS My Irish paternal grandmother, who married my grandfather Gerard after eloping with him and breaking all ties with her family.

ROSSANA Andreina and Beppino's daughter and my oldest friend.

THE SFORZA DYNASTY Founded in the fourteenth century by Muzio Attendolo, and subsequently renamed Sforza (from "*sforzare*," meaning to exert or force). His successors, including Ludovico Sforza, Duke of Milan, went on to become some of the most powerful members of the Italian aristocracy.

SOPHIE MARKARION One of the many Armenian women who Valentine and Germaine rescued from Turkey and went on to become a family friend in Paris, where she made orange cordial in the bidet. She was married to Gabriel Markarion.

STEVE My eldest brother.

VALENTINA, THE MYSTERIOUS RUSSIAN ANCESTRESS The infamous, glamorous Russian ancestress, who apparently my grandmother and I were named after.

INDEX